"THE HIGHER CHRISTIAN LIFE"

SOURCES FOR THE STUDY OF THE HOLINESS, PENTECOSTAL, AND KESWICK MOVEMENTS

*A forty-eight-volume
facsimile series reprinting
extremely rare documents for the study of
nineteenth-century religious and social history,
the rise of feminism, and the history of the
Pentecostal and Charismatic movements*

Edited by
Donald W. Dayton
Northern Baptist Theological Seminary

Advisory Editors
D. William Faupel, *Asbury Theological Seminary*
Cecil M. Robeck, Jr., *Fuller Theological Seminary*
Gerald T. Sheppard, *Union Theological Seminary*

A GARLAND SERIES

THE
HIGHER
CHRISTIAN LIFE

A Bibliographical Overview

with a Preface by
Donald W. Dayton
Northern Baptist
Theological Seminary

Garland Publishing, Inc.
New York & London
1985

For a complete list of the titles in this series
see the final pages of this volume.

Library of Congress Cataloging-in-Publication Data
Main entry under title:

The Higher Christian life.

("The Higher Christian life")
Reprint (1st work). Originally published: Wilmore,
Ky. : B.L. Fisher Library, Asbury Theological Seminary,
1971. (The First Occasional bibliographic papers of the
B.L Fisher Library)
Reprint (2nd work). Originally published: Wilmore,
Ky. : B.L. Fisher Library, Asbury Theological Seminary,
1972. (The Second Occasional bibliographic papers of the
B.L. Fisher Library)
Reprint (3rd work). Originally published: Wilmore,
Ky. : B.L. Fisher Library, Asbury Theological Seminary,
1975. (The Third Occasional bibliographic papers of the
B.L. Fisher Library)
Includes index.
Contents: The American Holiness movement / Donald W.
Dayton — The American Pentecostal movement / David W.
Faupel — Keswick / David D. Bundy.
1. Holiness churches—United States—Bibliography.
2. Pentecostalism—United States—Bibliography.
3. Pentecostal churches—United States—Bibliography.
4. Keswick movement—Bibliography.   5. United States—
Church history—Bibliography.   I. Dayton, Donald W.
American Holiness movement, 1985.   II. Faupel, David W.
American Pentecostal movement.   1985.   II. Faupel, David W.
American Pentecostal movement.   1985.   III. Bundy, David
David D. Keswick.   1985   IV. Series.   V. Series:
Occasional bibliographic papers of the B.L. Fisher
Library ; 1st–3rd.
Z7845.H6H54   1985   016.2773'08   85-20764
[BX7990.H6]
ISBN 0-8240-6400-3 (alk. paper)

CONTENTS

PREFACE

Among the most powerful but also among the least well understood of modern religious movements have been the variety of "higher Christian life" currents that have swept the world in the wake of the nineteenth-century "holiness revival." Born in the antebellum American synthesis of newly imported Methodist doctrines of "Christian perfection" with the emerging "new measures" revivalism of evangelist Charles Grandison Finney, this holiness revival in its ripple effect has not only been one of the most determinative factors in the shaping of American popular religious life but has also produced literally scores of denominations in North America alone. Through aggressive missionary activity of its advocates this movement has circled the globe and shaped religious life around the world. In the twentieth century a radical wing of this movement evolved into Pentecostalism and since the 1960s into the "neo-Pentecostal" or "charismatic movement" that has permeated most major Christian bodies and become one of the most notable religious forces in the modern world.

In spite of this impact these religious currents are not well understood. There are many reasons for this. American religious history has all too often been interpreted through the academic theological traditions that have not represented what was occurring on the level of popular piety. Reflecting this orientation the academic libraries have not collected the materials relevant to this area of study, and as a result it is almost impossible for scholars to trace the themes and interconnections of these religious movements. Only very recently have the various denominations spawned by these currents begun to come to historical consciousness, and when they do they often cultivate only the small part of the historical sources related most directly to their own history. And, most interestingly, as these groups enter the mainstream of American religious life, there has been a tendency to assimilate to the more dominant patterns and in the process even suppress the actual character of their own roots in favor of a historiography offering a supposedly more respectable lineage.

This series is intended to help rectify this situation on several levels. It hopes to provide the basic sources, often very scarce and thus unavailable, that will enable students of American religion to understand the emergence of these currents and the dynamics that have motivated them—and thus fill in a major gap in American religious history. It intends to display the variety and interconnections of the various aspects of the movements so that the basic configurations will be discernible and the most important developments can be understood. Making this material more accessible to the academic world will hopefully contribute to a profounder understanding of the nineteenth century, will illuminate recent religious developments in the twentieth century, and will require the revision of many accepted scholarly conclusions.

Many of the popular social movements of the nineteenth century cannot be understood, for example, without attention to this material. Recent scholarship has revealed the extent to which the antislavery movement was rooted in antebellum perfectionist revivalism, but there are still only hints in the literature of the extent to which the feminist movement of the nineteenth century was itself carried by the perfectionist currents. Only when the materials made available in this series are fully digested will the dynamic behind the rise of feminism be clear. (This thesis is argued in more detail in the introduction to volume 11, *Holiness Tracts Defending the Ministry of Women*.) Other social currents of the nineteenth centry (prohibition, dietary reform, slum mission and social work, the struggle against the "white slave trade" and prostitution, etc.) are all illuminated by the material included in this series of reprints.

Robert Mapes Anderson has suggested in his study of Pentecostalism, *The Vision of the Disinherited* (Oxford University Press, 1979), that the historiography of American "fundamentalism" and "evangelicalism" will remain distorted until an understanding of these currents is fully integrated into such study. Scholarly attention has turned within the last decade or so more fully to the study of the so-called "evangelicalism," perceived now in the twentieth century as outside the mainstream of American culture, but much of this work is vitiated by its lack of attention to the themes represented in this series. Even though much of the modern "evangelical" culture and institutions are rooted in these currents, categories of interpretation are derived from historiographies and dynamics foreign to the phenomena themselves. Only when the material of this series is fully incorporated into the historiography of evangelicalism will the contemporary religious scene be fully understood.

This fact could be illustrated on several levels, but a few examples will have to suffice. The "electronic church" that has become highly visible in our culture is dominated by independent evangelists with roots in the Pentecostal experience. The material in this series is chosen to illuminate the themes of these currents: the experience of "baptism in the Holy Spirit," the practice of "speaking in tongues," the advocacy of "faith healing," and so forth. The modern charismatic movement is best understood as a more moderate articulation of these themes qualified by the more traditional theologies and practices of the established churches. Recent Gallup polls have revealed the astonishing extent to which such themes shape the religious life of the American populace. This series of reprints will enable scholars to understand the historical roots and religious and theological dynamics of these themes.

This series is based on a broad understanding of the nature and significance of the holiness revival of the nineteenth century as it found expression in a bewildering variety of currents that may be roughly grouped into three basic movements or traditions: (1) the holiness movement proper, distinguished by its effort to maintain an American variation on the Methodist doctrine of "entire sanctification" as a "second blessing"—a concern that led by the end of the nineteenth century to the founding of a large number of churches that have since come together in the Christian Holiness Association to form a self-conscious tradition of American Christianity; (2) the Keswick movement, named for summer conventions held in the lake district town of Keswick in England, which represents a more moderate form of the teaching that emphasized the "deeper" or "victorious" Christian life and found expression not only in a number of church bodies, but also in interdenominational missionary movements and the piety of many beyond the strict institutional confines of the churches spawned by the movement; and (3) the Pentecostal movement, a radicalization of the other two currents at the turn of the century advocating the recovery of charismatic gifts, especially "speaking in tongues," and produced in time an extended network of denominations, major missionary movements, and ultimately the charismatic movement.

The reprints in this series are drawn from a period that is not well documented. The earlier roots of the movements within Methodism can be more easily controlled because the sources of classical Methodism have been well collected and analyzed. And Pentecostalism began to receive broader cultural attention in the 1920s and 1930s. This collection concentrates on the period in between, roughly a hundred-year period beginning in the 1830s.

PREFACE

This volume, intended to serve as an introduction to the series, provides a bibliographical overview of the movements under consideration by reprinting three pioneering bibliographical essays. The first two, that by Donald W. Dayton on the holiness movement and that by David W. Faupel on Pentecostalism, were originally presented as papers to the annual convention of the American Theological Library Association in a series of bibliographical introductions to various American ecclesiastical traditions. Together they provide an overview of the larger body of material from which the selections for this series have been chosen. The essays are printed without change except for some minor excisions of dated material and the addition of an integrated index of names prepared by my student assistant Chuck Westerman for this volume.

In terms of detail the essays reprinted in this volume have now been superceded by two massive bibliographical guides prepared by Charles E. Jones, *A Guide to the Study of the Holiness Movement* (Metuchen, NJ: Scarecrow Press, 1974) and *A Guide to the Study of the Pentecostal Movement* in two volumes (Metuchen, NJ: Scarecrow Press, 1983), both published in the bibliography series of the American Theological Library Association. Advanced scholars in the area will turn constantly to these volumes, but the essays reprinted in this volume provide a more accessible overview. The most useful historical overview of the nineteenth-century holiness revival at this time is Melvin E. Dieter, *The Holiness Revival of the Nineteenth Century* (Metuchen, NJ: Scarecrow Press, 1980) and the story of the emergence of Pentecostalism from the holiness revival is told in Donald W. Dayton, *Theological Roots of Pentecostalism* (Metuchen, NJ: Scarecrow Press, 1986), both volumes in the Monograph series, "Studies in Evangelicalism." The most useful survey of modern Pentecostalism is now Robert Mapes Anderson, *Vision of the Disinherited: The Making of American Pentecostalism* (New York: Oxford University Press, 1979).

Donald W. Dayton
Northern Baptist
Theological Seminary

THE AMERICAN HOLINESS MOVEMENT

A BIBLIOGRAPHIC INTRODUCTION

1

THE AMERICAN HOLINESS MOVEMENT

A BIBLIOGRAPHIC INTRODUCTION

by

Donald W. Dayton

The First in a Series of
"Occasional Bibliographic Papers
of the B.L. Fisher Library"

B.L. Fisher Library
Asbury Theological Seminary
Wilmore, Kentucky 40390
1971

4

Price

1 - 4 copies $2.00 each
5 or more copies $1.50 each

plus postage and handling
unless payment accompanies order.

Preface

This paper was first presented to the twenty-fifth
annual conference of the American Theological
Library Association in June, 1971. Each year the
Association attempts to provide a bibliographic
paper relating to the theological tradition of the
institution at which the annual conference is held.
This paper is then printed in the PROCEEDINGS of
the Association and serves as a guide for library
acquisitions in the member schools.

The 1971 Conference was held at Pasadena College,
Pasadena, California, a denominational college of
the Church of the Nazarene. Dr. Genevieve Kelly,
then vice-president and program chairman of the
Association, requested a paper on the American
Holiness Movement. Since so little has been done
in this area, I prepared a paper of broader orientation than some in the series in the hope that it
could also serve to introduce others to this
neglected facet of the American Church. A number
of those present at the Conference requested that
the paper be made available to a wider readership
than that of the PROCEEDINGS of the Association.
This booklet is presented in response to those
requests. No attempt has been made to revise the
paper. Only minor, and primarily stylistic,
changes have been made. Local references and the
oral style have been retained.

The library faculty of the B.L. Fisher Library
hope that this paper will be only the first in a
series of "Occasional Bibliographic Papers of the
B.L. Fisher Library." Such papers would present
in similar format other bibliographic projects of
faculty and friends of Asbury Theological Seminary.

I would like to express appreciation to the Rev.
David J. Wartluft, executive secretary of the

American Theological Library Association, for
granting permission to reprint this paper from the
PROCEEDINGS; to Mrs. Esther Richter, the library
secretary-receptionist, who typed two drafts of
this paper from a difficult manuscript; to Mrs.
Robert Lyon who prepared the final copy for printing; and especially to Mr. Frank Dewey, my student
assistant, who checked all the references and did
much of the proofreading. I take all responsibility for any errors and would be pleased to be
informed of any that are noticed.

Donald W. Dayton
Acquisitions Librarian and
    Assistant Professor of
    Bibliography and Research
B.L. Fisher Library
Asbury Theological Seminary

6

Contents

7

The American Holiness Movement:
A Bibliographic Introduction

Toward a Definition

Before I can introduce you "bibliographically" to
the American Holiness Movement, I must propose
some sort of definition. For some time it
appeared that you might not have this paper because of my inability to clear this first hurdle.
Here we are not dealing with a single denomination
or even with a precisely delimited tradition. The
picture is infinitely more complex. Let me strive
for an adequate definition by first presenting a
short sketch of the main thrust of the movement,
then by indicating some of the variations, and
finally by contrasting this resulting picture with
related movements.

Most of us have at least some awareness of the
turmoil on the American scene during the first
half of the 19th century and of the rise in the
churches of perfectionism, abolitionism, revivalism, etc. Out of this we wish to pick up one
thread. In the 1830's two sisters, Sarah Lankford
and Phoebe Palmer, members of New York City
Methodist churches, organized a weekly prayer
meeting which lasted into the 1900's and became
widely known as the "Tuesday Meeting." This meeting became a center of revival within Methodism
(and to some extent beyond the limits of this
denomination) of the original Wesleyan teaching of
sanctification as a second crisis in the Christian
life in which the believer gained victory over sin.
Phoebe Palmer left her own distinctive cast on this
doctrine by emphasizing that all Christians should

immediately enter into this experience.

In the late 1850's and the following decades, as a part of the general revival of that period,[1] there was a "holiness revival" inspired and fired by the "Tuesday Meeting" and other similar groups. In the late 1860's was founded a "National Camp Meeting Association for the Promotion of Holiness" which evolved over the years into the National Holiness Association (NHA) just renamed in April the Christian Holiness Association (CHA). Toward the end of the last century this movement came more and more into conflict with Methodist leadership. Out of many small groups and state "holiness" associations that had grown up, there evolved, usually by a complex series of mergers, separate

---

[1]. J. Edwin Orr has proposed that we speak of a "Second Evangelical Awakening" in 1857-59 that had such world-wide impact over the next 50 years that it may be compared with the 18th century awakening. If this thesis can be substantiated, then the American Holiness Movement would be that part of this awakening that operated within a "Wesleyan" context. Orr's thesis is defended in his Oxford doctoral dissertation published as THE SECOND EVANGELICAL AWAKENING IN BRITAIN (London: Marshall, Morgan & Scott, 1948) and also in his Northern Baptist Th.D. dissertation published as THE SECOND EVANGELICAL AWAKENING IN AMERICA (London: ?, 1953). These are summarized and popularized in THE SECOND EVANGELICAL AWAKENING (London: Marshall, Morgan & Scott, 1955). More accessible is his THE LIGHT OF THE NATIONS: EVANGELICAL RENEWAL AND ADVANCE IN THE NINETEENTH CENTURY (Grand Rapids: Eerdmans, 1965), which is more general and gives less attention to the development of this particular thesis.

holiness denominations such as the Church of the Nazarene[2] and the Pilgrim Holiness Church.[3] The implications of this growing split are not yet entirely realized. We must, therefore, speak of a movement still in process, but at least for the moment we will describe the American holiness movement as a loosely connected group both within and without Methodism that holds to a primitive Wesleyan position of "second blessing" holiness as shaped on the American scene by such forces as the

---

2. This sequence of events is chronicled in Charles Edwin Jones, "Perfectionist Persuasion: A Social Profile of the National Holiness Movement with American Methodism, 1867-1936." (unpublished Ph.D. dissertation, University of Wisconsin, 1968). Pages 557-567 are an extensive bibliography of materials relating to this denomination. The standard history is now Timothy Smith's excellent CALLED UNTO HOLINESS (Kansas City, Mo.: Nazarene Publishing House, 1962). The Church of the Nazarene has now over a third of a million members and well over twice that in Sunday School enrollment (plus another 100,000 overseas).

3. The Pilgrim Holiness Church merged in 1968 with the Wesleyan Methodist Church to form the Wesleyan Church, a denomination now numbering about 82,000 in the U.S.A. and half again as many in the rest of the world. Some account of the history is given in the Jones dissertation (note 2) where pages 571-577 consist of a bibliography relating to the Pilgrim Holiness Church. I am told that a history of the Pilgrims up to merger exists in a manuscript by Paul W. Thomas. A summary history may be found in the final issue of the PILGRIM HOLINESS ADVOCATE (June 29, 1968, incorrectly numbered vol. XLVII #13--actually vol. XLVIII #13).

American camp-meeting and the holiness revival at the time of the Civil War.

This is the main thread, but the stitching is infinitely more complicated. In the first place, at least two denominations presently affiliated with the CHA came into being before the "holiness revival." These arose before the Civil War in the "burned over" district of Western New York State. The Wesleyan Methodist Church[4] was founded in 1842 out of the abolitionist controversy within Methodism, and the Free Methodist Church[5] was founded in

---

4. As mentioned above (note 3) the Wesleyan Methodist Church merged with the Pilgrim Holiness Church in 1968 to form the Wesleyan Church. The history of the Wesleyan branch is chronicled in Roy S. Nicholson's revision (3rd edition) of Ira Ford McLeister's HISTORY OF THE WESLEYAN METHODIST CHURCH OF AMERICA (Marion, Ind.: Wesley Press, 1959) which I understand is being updated by Dr. Nicholson to the time of merger. Other bibliography is given on pages 518-9 of the Jones thesis mentioned previously. It should be noted that the Arno Press of the New York Times has recently reprinted in its series "Anti-Slavery Crusade in America" a book from the controversy surrounding the founding of the Wesleyans: Orange Scott, THE GROUNDS OF SECESSION FROM THE M.E. CHURCH (New York: C. Prindle, 1848; reprinted 1969).

5. This split is justified by B.T. Roberts in WHY ANOTHER SECT (Rochester: "The Earnest Christian" Publishing House, 1879) which consists primarily of response to articles in Bishop Simpson's CYCLOPEDIA OF METHODISM. The standard "interpretive history" of Free Methodism is Bishop Leslie Marston's FROM AGE TO AGE A LIVING WITNESS

1860 when its leaders were expelled from the
Genesee Conference of the Methodist Episcopal
Church. Both of these groups were then swept more
into the holiness orbit during the Holiness
Revival.

Secondly, the influence of the Holiness Revival
extended far beyond the boundaries of Methodism.
Two Mennonite groups, the Missionary Church[6] and
the Brethren in Christ,[7] and quite a number of

(Winona Lake, Ind.: Light and Life Press, 1960).
Other bibliography is provided on pages 568-569 of
the Jones thesis. The origins of the denomination
are being restudied by James Reinhard of Greenville
College (Illinois) for his doctoral program at
Iowa. Free Methodists now number about 65,000 in
the U.S.A. (nearly double this in Sunday School
enrollment) and another 60,000 abroad.

6. The Missionary Church was formed in 1969 by
    union of the Missionary Church Association and
the United Missionary Church (formerly the Menno-
nite Brethren in Christ). There is a small history
of the former branch by Walter H. Lugibihl and
Jared F. Gerig, THE MISSIONARY CHURCH ASSOCIATION
(Berne, Ind.: Economy Printing Concern, 1950).
The latter branch is treated in an earlier anthology edited by Jasper A. Huffman entitled HISTORY
OF THE MENNONITE BRETHREN IN CHRIST CHURCH (New
Carlisle, Ohio: Bethel Pub. Co., 1920). There is
also a later attempt by Everek Richard Storms,
HISTORY OF THE UNITED MISSIONARY CHURCH (Elkhart,
Ind.: Bethel Pub. Co., 1958). The new denomina-
tion has a membership of about 20,000 members and
a Sunday School enrollment of about 40,000.

7. The Brethren in Christ (formerly known as the
    "River Brethren") are popularly known because

"Friends,"[8] were caught up in the Holiness Revival, adopted Wesleyan views and are now members of the CHA. Other groups, such as the Christian and

---

of President Eisenhower's youthful association with this group. They are closely related to the groups mentioned in note 6. There exists a history by Asa W. Climenhaga entitled HISTORY OF THE BRETHREN IN CHRIST CHURCH (Nappanee, Ind.: E.V. Pub. House, 1942), but this account has been called into question at a number of points. See, for example, "The Origin of the Brethren in Christ Church and its Later Divisions" by Ira D. Landis in MENNONITE QUARTERLY REVIEW, XXXIV (October, 1960), 290-307. Carlton O. Wittlinger, Archivist for the denomination, is, I understand, preparing a new history. Preliminary studies have appeared in NOTES AND QUERIES IN BRETHREN IN CHRIST HISTORY, published by the Archives in Grantham, Pa. The denomination currently numbers about 10,000 in American membership and twice that in Sunday School enrollment.

8. Four yearly meetings of Friends--Ohio, Rocky Mountain, Northwest (formerly Oregon) and Kansas--have grouped themselves together as the Evangelical Friends Alliance. All of these have been influenced by the Holiness Revival but only the first two of these maintain separate membership in the CHA. Walter R. Williams provides some of the historical background of these groups in his THE RICH HERITAGE OF QUAKERISM (Grand Rapids: Eerdmans, 1962). A few further items of bibliography are given in pages 517-518 of the Jones thesis (note 2). I am unable to locate statistics for all of these groups. In 1970 the Ohio Yearly Meeting reported a membership of about 7,500 and a Sunday School enrollment of nearly 9,000.

Missionary Alliance[9] show the influence of the
movement even though they have never affiliated
with CHA.

A third variation may be seen in the Salvation
Army. Founder William Booth, a British Methodist,
came under the influence of American holiness
evangelist James Caughey. This movement came to
the U.S.A. in the 1880's and has since identified
with the CHA.[10]

---

9. The Christian & Missionary Alliance originated
    in the 1880's under the leadership of New York
City Presbyterian minister A.B. Simpson out of his
concern for missions and the disenfranchised. The
founder's life has been chronicled by A.E. Thompson,
A.B. SIMPSON: HIS LIFE AND WORK (Rev. ed.,
Harrisburg, Pa.: Christian Publications, 1939).
Some historical information is also embedded in
the interpretative study of Samuel Stoesz, UNDER-
STANDING MY CHURCH (Harrisburg, Pa.: Christian
Publications, 1968). The 75th anniversary volume
is devoted entirely to chronicling the mission
works: J.H. Hunter, BESIDE ALL WATERS (Harrisburg,
Pa.: Christian Publications, 1964). The latest
edition of the MISSIONARY ATLAS (Harrisburg, Pa.:
Christian Publications, 1964) is the fourth in a
series. The inclusive membership in North America
numbered about 120,000 in 1969 while world-wide
was about three times that figure.

10. The definitive history of the Salvation Army
     is, of course, THE HISTORY OF THE SALVATION
ARMY (London: Nelson, 1947-) of which 5 volumes
are now complete (the first three by Robert
Sandall, the last two by Arch Wiggins). Designed
for popular consumption, but centering on the work
of the Army in America, is Sallie Chesham, BORN TO
BATTLE: THE SALVATION ARMY IN AMERICA (Chicago:

Fourthly, in the basic pattern which produced the
Nazarenes and the Pilgrim Holiness Church, there
were spawned, especially around the turn of the
century, a large number of other groups that have
not become affiliated with the CHA. The largest
of these is the Church of God (Anderson, Indiana)[11]
founded in 1881 by D.S. Warner. They rejected
entirely the idea of an organized denomination and
withdrew from the national association because of
its implicit acceptance of such groups.

And finally certain events in the Twentieth century have produced small off-shoots of Methodism
that have identified with the CHA. Among these
have been the Evangelical Methodist Church[12]

Rand McNally, 1965). Neither of these gives much
attention to the relation of the Salvation Army
to the holiness movement. It was in the person
of Samuel Logan Brengle, especially at the turn
of the century, that this relationship developed.
THE YEARBOOK OF AMERICAN CHURCHES (1971) reports
inclusive membership of 331,711 for this group.

11. The history of this group has been chronicled
    at least twice, by Charles E. Brown, WHEN THE
TRUMPET SOUNDED: A HISTORY OF THE CHURCH OF GOD
REFORMATION MOVEMENT (Anderson, Ind.: Warner
Press, 1951) and John W.V. Smith, TRUTH MARCHES
ON: A BRIEF STUDY OF THE HISTORY OF THE CHURCH OF
GOD REFORMATION MOVEMENT (Anderson, Ind.: Gospel
Trumpet Co., 1956). This group reported in 1969
nearly 150,000 members and a Sunday School enroll-
ment of nearly 250,000.

12. There is as yet no major history of this
    denomination. A short historical sketch was
included in the papers of the Study Conference on
Federation of Holiness Churches sponsored by the

founded in 1946 in reaction to liberal trends
within Methodism and the Evangelical Church of
North America[13] founded after the 1968 merger of
the Methodist and Evangelical United Brethren
Churches. It will be obvious that different dynamics are at work here, but because of their conservative Methodist orientation, these groups
identify with the CHA.

This then is what we shall mean by the American
holiness movement.[14] Total American membership of

NHA in Chicago, Nov. 30 - Dec. 2, 1966. Of some
value is the autobiography of the founder J.H.
Hamblen, A LOOK INTO LIFE (Abilene, Texas: J.H.
Hamblen, 1969). Current membership is about
10,000.

13. This denomination consists primarily of
     churches from the Evangelical United Brethren,
especially the Pacific Northwest and Montana conferences, as well as churches in the Mississippi
Valley and Western Pennsylvania. It now includes
more than 100 congregations.

14. Other groups both within the CHA and without
     could be mentioned, but the line had to be
drawn somewhere. And of necessity I have used the
present membership of the CHA as a guideline, mentioning only the largest and most significant
groups outside. For the sake of completeness I
should include two other small denominations that
do hold CHA membership. The largest of these,
numbering in 1969 about 8,000 members and twice
that in Sunday School enrollment, is the Churches
of Christ in Christian Union, founded in 1909
although its roots go back to Civil War days.
Little seems to be available about them except THE
CHURCHES OF CHRIST IN CHRISTIAN UNION: HISTORY,

these churches (excluding the Christian and Missionary Alliance) would number about one million, though this number is somewhat deceptive. Rather strict membership requirements and vigorous programs of outreach (especially the Sunday School) mean that the actual constituency is probably twice or more the membership. To this total must be added a significant, but decreasing, number of Methodists who would still identify with Methodist institutions, camp meetings, and churches highly influenced by the holiness movement within Methodism.

Much of the American Holiness Movement is loosely grouped together in the Christian Holiness Association. Unity is found primarily in a common commitment to the Wesleyan view of "full salvation." For the most part the individual groups are young and vigorous and still in the process of moving from sect to church if we may use for convenience, Troeltsch's terms. In the neighborhood of 50 schools and colleges, several with graduate

---

ORGANIZATION, MISSIONS, WHAT WE TEACH (Circleville, Ohio: ?, 196?). The other group is the Holiness Christian Church, originally the Pennsylvania Conference of a larger church by this name which participated in the series of mergers producing the Pilgrim Holiness Church. Many other groups could be considered. These can be discovered and traced by use of Leslie Wilcox and Charles Jones (cf. infra under "Bibliography") and the earlier dissertation by Merrill Gaddis (cf. infra under "History"), as well as Elmer T. Clark, THE SMALL SECTS IN AMERICA (Nashville: Cokesbury Press, 1937). Since W.J. Hollenweger does not distinguish holiness from pentecostal groups, much information will be found in his 10 vol. HANDBUCH DER PFINGSTBEWEGUNG, available from the ATLA Board of Microtext.

programs, are affiliated with the CHA. Of particular interest to this group would be the three theological seminaries associated with the movement: Asbury Theological Seminary (founded 1923), the Nazarene Theological Seminary (1945), and Western Evangelical Seminary (1945). The first two are accredited members of AATS, the third is an associate member.

Finally, I wish to distinguish the American Holiness Movement from three related movements: the Keswick Movement, Pentecostalism, and Methodism.

It should be noted first of all that there are in American thought and history many other expressions of holiness and Christian Perfectionism. Among these would be especially revivalist Charles Finney and Asa Mahan within Congregationalism.[15]

----

15. Finney's LECTURES ON REVIVALS OF RELIGION
    (Cambridge: Belknap Press of Harvard U.P., 1960) exist in a critical edition edited by William G. McLoughlin. Other works of importance for the holiness movement that have been kept in print include his LECTURES ON SYSTEMATIC THEOLOGY (Grand Rapids: Eerdmans, 1951) and SANCTIFICATION (London: Christian Literature Crusade, 1950). There is also an edition of his notes for students entitled SKELETONS OF A COURSE OF THEOLOGICAL LECTURES ON THEOLOGY (Minneapolis: Bethany Fellowship, 1968). His MEMOIRS have been kept in print by Revell as the AUTOBIOGRAPHY. Seven volumes of his sermons were published five years ago as "The Charles G. Finney Memorial Library" by Kregel. McLoughlin's introduction to the Lectures suggests bibliography for the life of Finney (p. XVI, pp. LVI - LIX, and p. 3). There is a popular "holiness" biography by Aaron Merritt Hills, LIFE OF CHARLES G. FINNEY (Cincinnati: Office of God's

The Oberlin School and Finney's revival techniques
have had great impact on the development of the
American holiness movement. Others in other denominations either came under the influence of the
Palmers' "Tuesday Meeting" or rose concurrently
with it preaching a similar message. Among these

Revivalist," 1902). Richard Taylor, perhaps the
most prominant holiness theologian today, offered
as his doctoral dissertation at Boston in 1953, a
study entitled "The Doctrine of Sin in the Theology of Charles Grandison Finney." It was Asa
Mahan, however, who was more directly appropriated
by the holiness movement. Mahan worked with the
Wesleyans in some projects. THE BAPTISM OF THE
HOLY GHOST was published by the Palmers and is
available today in reprint from both H.E. Schmul
and Newby Book Room. Schmul has also reprinted in
paperback his MISUNDERSTOOD TEXTS OF SCRIPTURE
EXPLAINED AND ELUCIDATED, AND THE DOCTRINE OF THE
HIGHER LIFE THEREBY VERIFIED and in hardback his
CHRISTIAN PERFECTION. Mahan left two major auto-
biographical statements, the AUTOBIOGRAPHY (London:
T. Woolmer, 1882) and the more devotional OUT OF
DARKNESS, INTO LIGHT (various editions). There is
almost no secondary literature on Mahan. Robert S.
Fletcher's two volume HISTORY OF OBERLIN COLLEGE
(Oberlin: Oberlin College, 1943) is important for
both Finney and Mahan. About 200 pages are
devoted to these men in Vol. II of Benjamin B.
Warfield's fiercely polemical PERFECTIONISM (New
York: Oxford U.P., 1931). These were originally
journal articles and are very important bibliographically in studying the Oberlin School as well
as the other figures about to be mentioned in the
background to the Keswick movement. All of the
essays of interest here except the one on Thomas
Upham have been reissued in one volume by
Presbyterian & Reformed Pub. Co. (1958).

were Congregationalist Thomas Upham,[16] professor
at Bowdoin and the first male to enter the hal-
lowed precincts of the "Tuesday Meeting," Baptist
evangelist A.B. Earle,[17] Quakers David Updegraff
and Dougan Clark,[18] and Presbyterians W.E.
Boardman[19] and R. Pearsall Smith and his wife

---

16. Thomas C. Upham's PRINCIPLES OF THE INTERIOR
     OR HIDDEN LIFE (Boston: D.S. King, 1843) was
the only title by a non-Methodist in a series of
"Abridged Holiness Classics" published by the
Nazarenes in the 1940's. He is also known for his
life of Madame Guyon, frequently reprinted. These
and other works are analyzed by George Peck, "Dr.
Upham's Works," in THE METHODIST QUARTERLY REVIEW,
XXVIII (1846), 248-265. Warfield devoted over 100
pages to him in Vol. II of the original edition of
PERFECTIONISM (cf. note 15).

17. Author of THE REST OF FAITH (Boston: J.H.
     Earle, 1867) and an autobiography, BRINGING
IN SHEAVES (Boston: J.H. Earle, 1868).

18. A selection of Updegraff's sermons were pub-
     lished as OLD CORN, OR SERMONS AND ADDRESSES
ON THE SPIRITUAL LIFE (Boston: McDonald and Gill,
1892). His life story is told by Dougan Clark and
Joseph H. Smith, DAVID B. UPDEGRAFF AND HIS WORK
(Cincinnati: published for Smith by the
"Revivalist," 1895). Clark of Earlham College
contributed several works to the holiness move-
ment. Among these were THE HOLY GHOST DISPENSA-
TION (Chicago: Assn. of Friends, 1891), THE
THEOLOGY OF HOLINESS (Boston: McDonald & Gill,
1893) and THE OFFICES OF THE HOLY SPIRIT (New
York: George Hughes, 1878).

19. His works include especially THE HIGHER
     CHRISTIAN LIFE (Boston: Henry Hoyt, 1859)

Hannah Whitall Smith.[20] All of these figures had
an impact on the holiness movement, but their
major impact was felt on what is now called the

_____

and his life is narrated by his wife, Mary M.
Boardman, LIFE AND LABORS OF REV. W.E. BOARDMAN
(New York: Appleton, 1886). Warfield gives
attention to the Boardmans in his treatment of the
"Higher Life" Movement (note 15).

20. Robert Pearsall Smith wrote HOLINESS THROUGH
     FAITH (Rev. ed.; New York: Anson D.F.
Randolph & Co., n.d.) among other works, but it
was his Quaker wife, Hannah Whitall Smith, who
produced THE CHRISTIAN'S SECRET OF A HAPPY LIFE
(London: 1875) which the publisher claimed in
1952 had sold over 2 million copies and has been
translated into most major languages. It is avail-
able in several editions from Revell. Moody Press
of Chicago has reprinted in paperback her EVERYDAY
RELIGION (1893) and the GOD OF ALL COMFORT (1906).
She wrote an autobiography, THE UNSELFISHNESS OF
GOD (New York: Revell, 1903). Her son Logan
Pearsall Smith, collected her letters in PHILA-
DELPHIA QUAKER (New York: Harcourt, Brace and Co.,
1950), first published in London as A RELIGIOUS
REBEL (London: Nisbet, 1949). Her granddaughter,
Rachel Strachey published under the pseudonym Ray
Strachey a selection of Hannah Whitall Smith's
papers dealing with various 19th century American
religious sects, RELIGIOUS FANATICISM (London:
Faber & Gwyer, 1928) on which she also based a
novel SHAKEN BY THE WIND (London: Faber & Gwyer,
1927 and New York: Macmillan, 1928). Warfield
gives much space to the Smiths and lists her books
on pp. 510-11 of the original edition of
PERFECTIONISM.

Keswick movement,[21] another "higher life" or victorious life" movement somewhat parallel to the Wesleyan holiness movement, but distinguished from it primarily by its context in Reformed theology and its emphasis on gradual rather than instantaneous sanctification.

We must also distinguish the American Holiness Movement from Pentecostalism.[22] This is not done

---

21. The Keswick Movement arose in England out of the work of Boardman and the Smiths and began about 1874 as a series of conventions. It was brought back to the U.S.A. when Moody invited its speakers to Northfield. The "authorized" history is J.C. Pollock's, THE KESWICK STORY (London: Hodder & Stoughton, 1964). Earlier treatments include Walter B. Sloan, THESE SIXTY YEARS (London: Pickering & Inglis, 1935) and Steven Barabas, SO GREAT SALVATION (Westwood, N.J.: Revell, 1952). The latter is particularly helpful, containing an exposition of the teaching, bibliography, biographical sketches. THE KESWICK CONVENTION and THE KESWICK WEEK carry the annual addresses in Britain. A number of these have been anthologized by Herbert F. Stevenson in KESWICK'S AUTHENTIC VOICE (Grand Rapids: Zondervan, 1959) and KESWICK'S TRIUMPHANT VOICE (Grand Rapids: Zondervan, 1963). Ernest R. Sandeen in his exciting ROOTS OF FUNDAMENTALISM (Chicago: U. of Chicago Press, 1970) treats briefly the transfer back to the U.S.A. and the subsequent impact on fundamentalism (pp. 172-181).

22. Pentecostal bibliography is an area worthy of study in its own right. I can only make a few preliminary suggestions. The usual introduction now is John Thomas Nichol, PENTECOSTALISM (New York: Harper & Row, 1966), originally a

in many treatments and is the cause of much confusion. It is true that Pentecostalism arose about the same time and as a result of some of the same social and theological forces at the turn of the century that produced the Nazarenes and the Pilgrim Holiness Church. A common emphasis on the work of the Holy Spirit led both to use the term "pentecostal." It was common among the Nazarenes, and at Asbury Seminary founder H.C. Morrison's paper was called the PENTECOSTAL HERALD. But when the word came to be associated with the experience of glossolalia, most holiness groups dropped it. The holiness movement represented by the CHA has consistently taken a strong stand against this

---

dissertation at Boston U. Included is a helpful, classified nine page bibliography. Nils Bloch-Hoell, THE PENTECOSTAL MOVEMENT (Oslo: Universitetsforlaget, 1964; also available from Allen & Unwin, London) provides European perspective and international bibliography in greater detail. The Catholic treatment by Prudencio Damboriena, S.J., TONGUES AS OF FIRE (Washington, D.C.: Corpus Books, 1969) has been well reviewed in some quarters, but is filled with errors (the names of many holiness leaders, for example, are misspelled). The bibliography is also mediocre. Extremely helpful is the exegetical study by Frederick Dale Bruner, A THEOLOGY OF THE HOLY SPIRIT: THE PENTECOSTAL EXPERIENCE AND THE NEW TESTAMENT WITNESS (Grand Rapids: Eerdmans, 1970), originally a Hamburg dissertation. The appendix contains documents relating to the development of the doctrine and an extensive and detailed 25 page bibliography. Of course, for individuals, denominations, and world-wide coverage, nothing can match the 10 volume HANDBUCH DER PFINGSTBEWEGUNG by Walter J. Hollenweger, available from the ATLA Board of Microtext and described in a flyer issued by them.

phenomenon. I would suggest that the term "holiness" be used to describe conservative, revivalistic Wesleyanism and "pentecostal" be used to describe these groups that see the baptism of the Holy Spirit accompanied by the experience of "speaking in tongues." This would make perfect sense out of the name Pentecostal Holiness Church,[23] the group with which Oral Roberts was formerly associated. This group does merge a holiness view of sanctification with a pentecostal view of glossolalia, but not all Pentecostal groups are Wesleyan or holiness in understanding. The Assemblies of God, for example, are more "baptistic."[24] I would also suggest that a

---

23. This group was studied for a 1948 Th.D. at Union in Virginia by Joseph E. Campbell. This subsequently became the "official" history as THE PENTECOSTAL HOLINESS CHURCH 1898-1948 (Franklin Springs, Ga.: Publishing House of the PHC, 1951). The origins were restudied at the University of Georgia (1967) by Harold Vinson Synan, THE PENTECOSTAL MOVEMENT IN THE UNITED STATES, which I understand Eerdmans has recently agreed to publish. Synan views Pentecostalism as a descendent from Methodism through the holiness movement. This reflects the perspective of his own denomination and is probably more true of the South in which his denomination is concentrated and which felt the impact of the holiness revival much later because of the movement's early association with abolitionism.

24. The term and the distinction are used by Klaude Kendrick, THE PROMISE FULFILLED (Springfield, Mo.: Gospel Publishing House, 1961), originally a dissertation in history at the University of Texas (1959). This is a standard history of Pentecostalism in the U.S.A. and

bibliographic paper on the branches of Pentecostalism would be of great value to ATLA members.

Finally I must relate the American Holiness Movement to American Methodism. This is, of course, much more complex. The holiness movement claims to be nothing more than primitive Wesleyanism and the true American successors of Wesley. There is much to support this claim, though it must be qualified because of the great impact on the movement of American revivalism and the camp meeting. For two or three decades the movement was, for the most part, within Methodism. The crisis came in the 1880's and 1890's. Successive splits have diluted the holiness movement within Methodism and strengthened the distinct groups. The gap has consistently widened and can be felt especially at such places as Asbury which tries to serve both groups. Until 1950 there had been only one non-Methodist president of NHA. Since 1950 all presidents have been from groups within the CHA. These trends will probably continue. But there is still a large segment of Methodism which relates to institutions identified with the holiness movement, especially in its more mature contemporary forms. Some have suggested that such forces as Methodism's move toward COCU or the rise of the conservative "Good News" movement in Methodism may produce eventually a large conservative "Wesleyan" church built around the core of the larger of the present holiness churches. Only time will tell, of course, what lies ahead.

---

and features the Assemblies of God. He also treats as "holiness-pentecostal" groups the Church of God (Cleveland, Tenn.) and the Church of God in Christ. Kendrick's eleven page bibliography should perhaps be mentioned.

Bibliography

I should perhaps remind you at this point that we
are dealing in many ways with a young movement
that until recently has had neither the time nor
the inclination to produce all the accouterments
of scholarship available in older movements or
denominations. Two of the seminaries are only a
quarter of a century old and the third would date
its major growth from the same period. It is not
possible for me to list and describe the various
time-honored, well-tested and reviewed sources. I
must instead indicate, sometimes informally, where
information is available.

For the earlier periods, of course, one may utilize
the Methodist sources. There has been in this
series a paper by Edward L. Fortney on "The History
and Literature of Methodism," ATLA Proceedings,
VIII (1954), 13-17. Asbury is now participating
in the projected Methodist Union Catalog and we
can anticipate that this will become thereby even
more helpful for study in this area. I should
also refer you to the bibliographies in various
scholarly treatments of the related 19th century
American movements. Exemplary of this type of
material would be the "Critical Essay on the
Sources of Information" in Timothy Smith, REVIVAL-
ISM AND SOCIAL REFORM (New York: Abingdon, 1957).

Little exists of the nature of separate bibliographies devoted specifically to the holiness movement. In October 1958, the NHA issued a small
eight-page, envelope-size "Bibliography on the
Deeper Life" which was intended as an "in-print"
list of "available books which present the doctrine
of the Deeper Christian Life from Arminian-Wesleyan
position." This list had been approved by the 90th
annual conference of the NHA in 1958.

Somewhat less than the title suggests, but still

helpful is the MASTER BIBLIOGRAPHY OF HOLINESS
WORKS (Kansas City, Mo.: Beacon Hill Press, 1965).
This was begun several years ago by Dr. Ross Price
at Pasadena, and was completed over the years at
the Nazarene Theological Seminary with the help of
a number of the faculty there. The NHA Bibliography was incorporated into this forty-five page
booklet containing about 700 titles. These are
divided into two groups, those that "promote
Christian holiness" (Part I) and "those related
treatises which provide suitable breadth in background reading." There is no attempt at classifi-
cation, annotation, or the indication of original
or varying editions. The last I knew this bibliography was available for the asking from the
Nazarene Theological Seminary.

Of more value in many ways, though not as complete,
is Leslie D. Wilcox, BE YE HOLY (Cincinnati: The
Revivalist Press, 1965). This originated as a
mimeographed syllabus for Dean Wilcox's classes at
God's Bible School in Cincinnati, and is now available in the second edition of the book form. This
book is most helpful. The first third consists of
a rather traditional statement of the position,
with its scriptural support and suggested readings
at each point. The other 270 pages are devoted to
history and bibliography of the movement. This
treatment starts with Wesley and puts the whole
movement in that context. Included are thumbnail
sketches of major groups, essays on doctrinal
development, introduction to the controversies
within the movement, etc.

Finally I would like to draw your attention to a
dissertation (already mentioned) by Charles E.
Jones, now of Houghton College, "Perfectionist
Persuasion: A Social Profile of the National
Holiness Movement Within American Methodism, 1867-
1936" (University of Wisconsin, 1968 - University
Microfilms order #68-9083). The degree could have

been awarded merely on the basis of the nearly 300 pages of appended material and bibliography! He includes charts showing denominational origins and inter-relationships, Camp Meeting sites and committees, a fifteen page list of present and past holiness schools with founding dates and all name changes, and one hundred and forty pages of classified bibliography.

It should perhaps be noted that serious bibliographic work on this movement has been available only in the last six years. This paper would have been impossible without these recent efforts.

History

The historian par excellence of the American Holiness Movement is Nazarene Timothy L. Smith of Johns Hopkins. He set the context of the movement in a book based on his Harvard dissertation, REVIVALISM AND SOCIAL REFORM IN MID-NINETEENTH-CENTURY AMERICA (New York: Abingdon, 1957), now a standard work. He picked up the story again in his official history of the Church of the Nazarene, CALLED UNTO HOLINESS (Kansas City, Mo.: Nazarene Publishing House, 1962). Any student of the movement must start with these books and have his path further indicated by the bibliographic treasures embedded in Smith's documentation. A shorter 20 page statement supplementing these accounts may be found in Vol. II of THE HISTORY OF AMERICAN METHODISM (New York: Abingdon, 1964), under the title "The Holiness Crusades" (pp. 608-627).

Three works are of importance in tracing the development of the doctrine of Christian Perfection within American Methodism. Most readily available is John Leland Peters, CHRISTIAN PERFECTION AND AMERICAN METHODISM (New York: Abingdon, 1956), originally a Yale dissertation. To this must be added two unpublished dissertations. M.E. Gaddis, "Christian Perfectionism in America" (Doctoral dissertation, University of Chicago, 1929) moves from New Testament times until the beginnings of the 20th century. Claude Thompson of Emory produced "The Witness of American Methodism to the Historical Doctrine of Christian Perfection" (Doctoral dissertation, Drew University, 1949) which sees in Methodism the source of all modern perfectionist movements.

C.E. Jones, "Perfectionist Persuasion," already repeatedly cited, indicates further bibliography on the social context (pp. 521-525) and Methodist backgrounds (pp. 526-531). Jones chronicles the events from the 1850's until the rise of the Church of the Nazarene and the Pilgrim Holiness Church, giving particular attention to social forces, and the impact of the camp meeting as an institution. Delbert Rose of Asbury Seminary provides a short history of the National Holiness Association as chapter two of his A THEOLOGY OF CHRISTIAN EXPERIENCE (Minneapolis: Bethany Fellowship, 1965), originally his Iowa dissertation in 1952 and actually a treatment of the life and thought of Joseph H. Smith, "A product of the NHA who became its chief expositor-evangelist." Use of this work is unfortunately made difficult by its lack of an index. Rose, the official historian of the CHA, is working now on the manuscript of the "official history." Also in progress is a "social history" of the American holiness movement by Melvin Dieter, General Secretary of Educational Institutions in the Wesleyan Church, as a part of his doctoral program at Temple University.

I have tried to indicate above, in the notes to the first section, the standard histories of denominations related to the holiness movement. Jones, "Perfectionist Persuasion," gives extended

references (pp. 556-579). I have attempted to
supplement this, giving above more detailed information where he is weak. He also provides references to histories of important camp meetings
(pp. 547-550), social agencies and educational
institutions (pp. 550-552) and holiness associations and interdenominationalism (pp. 552-555).
Special mention should perhaps be made of Percival
Wesche, "The Revival of the Camp-Meeting by the
Holiness Groups" (unpublished M.A. thesis, University of Chicago Divinity School, 1945) and Morris
S. Daniels, THE STORY OF OCEAN GROVE (New York:
Methodist Book Concern, 1919, available on micro-
film from University Microfilms). The history of
Asbury Seminary has been told three times, but the
only published narrative is by Howard F. Shipps of
Asbury as A SHORT HISTORY OF ASBURY THEOLOGICAL
SEMINARY (Wilmore, Ky.: Asbury Theological
Seminary, 1953).

Biography

For 19th century figures, the usual Methodist
sources are of much value. A few very early figures like Orange Scott and Timothy Merritt made it
into the Methodist Volume (VII) of the ANNALS OF
THE AMERICAN PULPIT (New York: R. Carter, 1865,
reprinted 1969 by the Arno Press of the New York
Times) edited by William B. Sprague. Of more
value is Bishop Matthew Simpson, CYCLOPEDIA OF
METHODISM (5th edition; Philadelphia: Louis H.
Everts, 1882). Carl Price, WHO'S WHO IN AMERICAN
METHODISM (New York: E.B. Treat, 1916) is still
of help for turn of the century figures. But by
the time Price and Simpson were supplemented by
Clinton T. Howell, PROMINENT PERSONALITIES IN
AMERICAN METHODISM (Birmingham, Ala.: Lowry Press,
1945), only very occasional entries are of inter-
est. Frederick DeLand Leete, METHODIST BISHOPS:
PERSONAL NOTES AND BIBLIOGRAPHY (Nashville:

Parthenon, 1948) is also of value for some 19th century figures.

The later periods are much leaner in sources. Occasionally the standard biographical sources will be of some value for outstanding figures, but one should turn first to Jones, "Perfectionist Persuasion." About 80 pages of his bibliography (pp. 583-660) are devoted to "personalities." For each of nearly 300 figures he lists the standard sources in which biographical information may be found, indicates their own works and notes any separate biographies that may exist. Some of the larger or older holiness denominations have produced anthologies about their leaders or founder. Richard Blews produced an excellent volume on the Free Methodist Bishops under the title MASTER WORKMEN (Winona Lake: Light and Life Press, 1939; centennial edition, 1960). The Nazarenes have produced C.T. Corbett, OUR PIONEER NAZARENES (Kansas City, Mo.: Nazarene Publishing House, 1958) and Basil Miller, OUT UNDER THE STARS: LIFE SKETCHES OF EARLY NAZARENE LEADERS (Kansas City, Mo.: Nazarene Publishing House, 1941).

Individual biographies are of course, numerous. Many are not scholarly, and often the concern is more with piety than history. Some of these have already been indicated. Orange Scott of the Wesleyans was treated in 2 volumes by his comrade in the abolitionist movement, Lucius C. Matlack, LIFE OF ORANGE SCOTT (New York: C. Prindle and L.C. Matlack, 1847-48). B.T. Roberts of the Free Methodists was studied by Clarence H. Zahniser, EARNEST CHRISTIAN (n.p., 1957), based on his dissertation at Pittsburgh, 1951. Shortly after her death in 1874, the life of Phoebe Palmer was published by Richard Wheatley, THE LIFE AND LETTERS OF MRS. PHOEBE PALMER (New York: W.C. Palmer, Jr., 1876). Ernest Wall provides a short and more recent treatment as "I Commend Unto You Phoebe,"

RELIGION IN LIFE, XXVI (Summer, 1957), 396-408.
Dr. W.C. Palmer wrote THE LIFE AND LETTERS OF
LEONIDAS L. HAMLINE D.D. (New York: Carlton and
Porter, 1866) while his life in turn was chron-
icled by George Hughes, THE BELOVED PHYSICIAN,
WALTER C. PALMER (New York: Palmer and Hughes,
1884). The life of John Inskip, president of the
National Holiness Association for its first 17
years, was told by the next president William
McDonald and John E. Searles, "I AM, O LORD,
WHOLLY AND FOREVER THINE," THE LIFE OF REV. JOHN
S. INSKIP (Boston: McDonald and Gill, 1885). We
have already mentioned Delbert Rose's treatment of
later president Joseph H. Smith (cf. supra under
History). The Salvation Army leader in America
has been treated by Clarence Hall, SAMUEL LOGAN
BRENGLE (Chicago: Salvation Army Supply and Pur-
chasing Dept., 1933) a popular holiness biography
which has gone through a number of printings and
is still available. Donald P. Brickley has considered the life and work of Nazarene founder
Phineas F. Bresee in MAN OF THE MORNING (Kansas
City, Mo.: Nazarene Publishing House, 1960), based
on his dissertation at Pittsburgh, 1958. Of the
Pilgrims, Martin Wells Knapp has been considered
by Aaron M. Hills, A HERO OF FAITH AND PRAYER
(Cincinnati: Mrs. M.W. Knapp, 1902) and SETH COOK
REES: THE WARRIOR-SAINT (Indianapolis: Pilgrim
Book Room, 1934) by his son, Paul S. Rees. The
founder of Asbury Theological Seminary was studied
by Percival A. Wesche, HENRY CLAY MORRISON:
CRUSADER SAINT (Berne, Ind.: Herald Press for
Asbury Theological Seminary, 1963), based on his
dissertation at Oklahoma U., 1955.

There is also in the holiness movement a genre of
literature that stands midway between theology and
biography. The holiness evangelist hopes to produce the changed life rather than a system of
doctrine. Theology is embedded in life and taught
by means of biography, autobiography or the

relating of religious experience. Many of the
examples cited above fall into this category. But
it is the anthologies which are perhaps more interesting. At least two of these were brought out by
Phoebe Palmer. The best known is probably PIONEER
EXPERIENCES: OR THE GIFT OF POWER RECEIVED BY
FAITH, ILLUSTRATED AND CONFIRMED BY THE TESTIMO-
NIES OF EIGHTY LIVES: WITNESSES OF VARIOUS DENOM-
INATIONS (New York: W.C. Palmer, Jr., 1868).
HOLINESS MISCELLANY (Philadelphia: National Pub-
lishing Assn. for the Promotion of Holiness, 1882)
records the "testimonies" of prominent holiness
leaders within Methodism. Perhaps the most popu-
lar was edited by S. Olin Garrison, FORTY WITNESSES
COVERING THE WHOLE RANGE OF CHRISTIAN EXPERIENCE
(New York: Hunt & Eaton, 1888). From the 20th
century, we have, among others, Bernie Smith,
FLAMES OF LIVING FIRE: TESTIMONIES TO THE EXPE-
RIENCE OF ENTIRE SANCTIFICATION (Kansas City, Mo.:
Beacon Hill, 1950). Similar, but not personal
statements, is Mrs. Clara McLeister, MEN AND WOMEN
OF DEEP PIETY (Syracuse: Wesleyan Methodist Publishing Association, 1920 - reprinted 1970 by Newby
Book Room) edited and published by well-known
holiness evangelist E.E. Shelhamer. Widely read,
reprinted, and translated has been James Gilchrist
Lawson, DEEPER EXPERIENCES OF FAMOUS CHRISTIANS
(Anderson, Ind.: Warner Press, 1911), still available and reprinted in paperback. These last two
books draw on the wider Christian tradition to
teach holiness lessons.

Theology

Holiness theology also presents a complicated and
variegated picture. The Holiness Movement empha-
sizes the classical Methodist works. Primary of
course is John Wesley, A PLAIN ACCOUNT OF CHRISTIAN
PERFECTION, consistently reprinted, but in various
formats, some of which have been somewhat mutilated.

A holiness collection of Wesley's sermons will usually include "On Sin in Believers" and "The Repentence of Believers" which are not a part of the standard forty-four usually published. Saintly John Fletcher is also to be noted. His CHECKS TO ANTINOMIANISM have been valued, while his essay on "The New Birth" has been frequently reprinted, as well as an extract from his last "Check" as FLETCHER ON PERFECTION. Adam Clarke's famous six volume commentary has been the standard for holiness exegesis and has been abridged recently by Ralph Earle of the Nazarene Seminary into one large volume as Adam Clarke, COMMENTARY ON THE HOLY BIBLE (Kansas City, Mo.: Beacon Hill, 1967). Chapter 12 of his CHRISTIAN THEOLOGY (available in reprint from H.E. Schmul) has often been reprinted as ENTIRE SANCTIFICATION. Richard Watson's THEOLOGICAL INSTITUTES is also highly regarded.

Almost all holiness systematic theologies are by Methodist writers. Two British efforts have found much use in the United States. These are William B. Pope A COMPENDIUM OF CHRISTIAN THEOLOGY (2nd Rev. ed.; London: Wesleyan Conference Office, 1877-80) in three volumes and J. Agar Beet, A MANUAL OF THEOLOGY (London: Hodder and Stoughton, 1906 - also New York, 1906), which also appeared in an abridged edition. American Methodism has provided from Vanderbilt, T.O. Summers, SYSTEMATIC THEOLOGY (Nashville: Southern Methodist Publishing House, 1888) and from Drew, Bishop Randolph S. Foster's 6 volume STUDIES IN THEOLOGY (New York: Hunt and Eaton, 1889-99), John Miley's two volume SYSTEMATIC THEOLOGY (New York: Methodist Book Concern, 1894) and Olin Curtis' THE CHRISTIAN FAITH (Cincinnati: Jennings & Graham, 1905) though Miley and Curtis have had mixed reception.[25] Still

---

25. Robert Chiles, THEOLOGICAL TRANSITION IN AMERICAN METHODISM: 1790-1935 (New York:

required in some courses of study is the short
volume by Amos Binney and Daniel Steele, BINNEY'S
THEOLOGICAL COMPEND IMPROVED (New York: Nelson
and Phillips, 1875). In the 19th century Wesleyan
Luther Lee attempted ELEMENTS OF THEOLOGY
(Syracuse: S. Lee, 1856). Two twentieth century
attempts have been made by Nazarenes A.M. Hills,
FUNDAMENTAL CHRISTIAN THEOLOGY (Pasadena, Calif.:
C.J. Kinne, 1931) in two volumes and H. Orton
Wiley, CHRISTIAN THEOLOGY (Kansas City, Mo.:
Nazarene Publishing House, 1940-1943). This three
volume work was abridged with Paul T. Culbertson
as INTRODUCTION TO CHRISTIAN THEOLOGY (Kansas City,
Mo.: Beacon Hill, 1947). Wiley has been standard,
but is cast in a scholastic mode with emphasis on
polemic against 19th century Calvinism. As far as

Abingdon, 1965) is extremely illuminating and most
helpful for tracing the vicissitudes of Methodist
theology on the American scene. He confirms the
reservations of certain holiness thinkers about
these two men by seeing in them a crucial turning
point in American Methodist theology. But as far
as I know Chiles' thesis has not found wide circulation in holiness theological circles, perhaps
because of his somewhat Barthian categories. Also
of help is an essay from within the perspective of
the Evangelical Congregational Church, a split from
within the background of the Evangelical United
Brethren Church. Joel Samuels, now of the Newberry
Library in Chicago, has provided us with a "Bibliography of Wesleyan-Arminian Theology," LIBRARY
BULLETIN (of the Evangelical Congregational School
of Theology), VI (October, 1965), 1-9. Samuels
draws attention to the work of S.J. Gamertsfelder,
SYSTEMATIC THEOLOGY (Harrisburg, Pa.: Evangelical
Publishing House, 1919) and others within this
tradition and adds further comments about Miley
and Curtis.

I know, nothing is imminent, and meanwhile the gap
has been partly filled with W.T. Purkiser (ed.)
EXPLORING OUR CHRISTIAN FAITH (Kansas City, Mo.:
Beacon Hill, 1960), an anthology apparently designed as a college text in which essays on various "loci" of theology are collected.

But systematics have not been the forte of the
holiness movement. Much more characteristic are
collections of addresses or camp-meeting sermons
and treatises on the doctrine of primary concern
to the movement. Perhaps the first of these of
interest was THE CHRISTIAN'S MANUAL: A TREATISE
ON CHRISTIAN PERFECTION WITH DIRECTIONS FOR OBTAIN-
ING THAT STATE (New York: Carlton & Porter, 1824)
by Timothy Merritt who founded THE GUIDE TO CHRIS-
TIAN PERFECTION. In 1841 George Peck, the editor
of THE QUARTERLY REVIEW, issued the SCRIPTURE
DOCTRINE OF CHRISTIAN PERFECTION (New York: Lane
and Sandford, 1842). Later there appeared a similar work by his brother, Jesse Peck, THE CENTRAL
IDEA OF CHRISTIANITY (Boston: H.V. Degen, 1856
issued in "Abridged Holiness Classic" series by
Beacon Hill, 1951, another shorter form available
in CHRISTIAN PERFECTION, a compilation of six holiness classics in one by H.E. Schmul). Of Phoebe
Palmer's many works should be mentioned the smaller
THE WAY OF HOLINESS (New York: Lane & Tippett,
1845) which went through 51 printings by 1871 and
the larger FAITH AND ITS EFFECTS (New York: Walter
C. Palmer, 1854). From the same period we should
mention LETTERS ON SANCTIFICATION or more properly
THE NECESSITY, NATURE AND FRUITS OF SANCTIFICATION
(New York: Lane & Scott, 1851) by Nathan Bangs,
one of the greatest leaders of 19th century
American Methodism.

A number of other Methodists made similar contributions. John A. Wood, who first suggested the
camp meeting association, wrote PERFECT LOVE
(Philadelphia: S.D. Burlock, 1861 - issued in

"Abridged Holiness Classics" series by Beacon
Hill, 1944 and recently reprinted by Newby) and
PURITY AND MATURITY (Boston: Christian Witness
Co., 1899 - issued in "Abridged Holiness Classics"
series by Beacon Hill, 1944). William McDonald,
second president of the National Campmeeting
Association, contributed among others THE SCRIP-
TURAL VIEWS OF HOLINESS (Philadelphia: National
Publishing Association for the Promotion of Holi-
ness, 1877). Bishop Randolph Foster produced
CHRISTIAN PURITY (New York: Harper and Brothers,
1851 - issued in the "Abridged Holiness Classics"
series by Beacon Hill, 1944 - another abridged
form now available in CHRISTIAN PERFECTION, six
holiness classics in one, by H.E. Schmul). Asbury
Lowry, who for some time edited THE CHRISTIAN
STANDARD wrote POSSIBILITIES OF GRACE (New York:
Phillips and Hunt, 1884 - issued in the "Abridged
Holiness Classics" series by Beacon Hill, 1944).
Near the turn of the century, Bishop Willard F.
Mallalieu contributed THE FULLNESS OF THE BLESSING
OF THE GOSPEL OF CHRIST (Cincinnati: Jennings and
Pye, 1903). T.O. Summers of Vanderbilt wrote
HOLINESS, A TREATISE ON SANCTIFICATION (Richmond:
J. Early, 1850). Perhaps the most significant
contributions were made by Daniel Steele, who
taught at both Syracuse and Boston. His works
have been constantly reprinted and include HALF
HOURS WITH ST. PAUL (Boston: Christian Witness
Co., 1895 - recently reprinted by Schmul), HALF
HOURS WITH ST. JOHN (Chicago: Christian Witness
Co., 1901 - recently reprinted by Schmul), MILE-
STONE PAPERS (New York: Eaton & Mains, 1876, later
enlarged - original edition recently reprinted by
Bethany Fellowship) containing his much referred
to defense of holiness from the Greek tenses, LOVE
ENTHRONED (Boston: Christian Witness Co., 1875 -
recently reprinted by Schmul), JESUS EXULTANT
(Boston: Christian Witness Co., 1899 - recently
reprinted by Schmul) and THE GOSPEL OF THE COMFORT-
ER (Boston: Christian Witness Co., 1897 -

recently reprinted by West Pub. Co., Apollo, Pa.).

Evangelists have also contributed much to the
holiness literature. Beverly Carradine from the
South wrote over twenty full-sized books. His
SECOND BLESSING IN SYMBOL (Columbia, S.C.: L.L.
Picket, 1893 - reprinted by Newby, 1968) illus-
trates the allegorical interpretation into which
holiness evangelists often fell. THE OLD MAN
(Louisville: Pentecostal Publishing Co., 1896 -
reprinted by Newby, 1965) raises in standard camp-
meeting terminology the problem of "inbred sin."
Others of his books deal more directly with sanctification. W.B. Godbey, best known for his COMMEN-
TARY ON THE NEW TESTAMENT (Cincinnati: Revivalist
Office, 1896-1900 and still available), also produced a number of other works including SANCTIFI-
CATION (Louisville: Kentucky Methodist Pub. Co.,
1896). Also an expositor and author of over
twenty books was George Watson, a Methodist who
later turned Wesleyan. Among his works was A
HOLINESS MANUAL (Boston: Christian Witness, Co.,
1882). S.A. Keen, asked by Methodist Bishops to
hold services in 76 different annual conference
sessions, produced half a dozen works, among them
FAITH PAPERS (Cincinnati: God's Revivalist, 1888 -
recently reprinted in full in CHRISTIAN PERFECTION,
six holiness classics in one, by H.E. Schmul).
And the list could be indefinitely extended in
terms of both authors and books.

The independent bodies have of course produced a
great deal of material. Free Methodist B.T.
Roberts' editorial writings in THE EARNEST CHRIS-
TIAN were compiled by his son Benson H. Roberts
as HOLINESS TEACHINGS (North Chili, N.Y.: Earnest
Christian Pub. House, 1893 - reprinted in paper-
back by Schmul, 1964). Much more recently Bishop
J. Paul Taylor contributed HOLINESS - THE FINISHED
FOUNDATION (Winona Lake, Ind.: Light and Life
Press, 1963 - also reissued in paperback). The

Wesleyans have produced a number of writers, but probably most interesting is Roy S. Nicholson, THE ARMINIAN EMPHASES (Owosso, Michigan: Owosso College, 196-). Dr. Nicholson was for years General Conference President. A founder of the Pilgrim Holiness Church and one of the most important figures of the turn of the century was Martin Wells Knapp, author of several books. Among these was OUT OF EGYPT INTO CANAAN: LESSONS IN SPIRITUAL GEOGRAPHY (Cincinnati: Cranston & Stowe, 1887 - recently reprinted by Book Nook, Box 2434, Phoenix, Arizona), a classical example of "Exodus" typology in holiness thought. From the Friends we have Everett Cattell of Malone College, THE SPIRIT OF HOLINESS (Grand Rapids: Eerdmans, 1963). Jasper A. Huffman of the United Missionary Church has produced a large number of books. Among them REDEMPTION COMPLETED (New Carlisle, Ind.: The Bethel Publishing Co., 1903) has gone through several editions. A 20th century classic was contributed by Englishman Harry E. Jessop who became Dean of the Chicago Evangelistic Institute (now Vennard College in Iowa). This widely used text is FOUNDATIONS OF DOCTRINE IN SCRIPTURE AND EXPERIENCE (Chicago: Chicago Evangelistic Institute, 1938 - still available from Vennard College, University Park, Iowa). Charles E. Brown of the Church of God (Anderson, Ind.) wrote the widely used THE MEANING OF SANCTIFICATION (Anderson, Ind.: The Warner Press, 1945 - recently reissued in paperback). Commissioner Samuel Logan Brengle of the Salvation Army left among others HELPS TO HOLINESS (New York: Salvation Army, 1918 - still available).

The Nazarenes have been by far the most prolific of the independent groups. From the 19th century we have the classic by A.M. Hills, originally a congregationalist who studied under Finney, HOLINESS AND POWER (Cincinnati: Revivalist Office, 1897 - still available). R.T. Williams wrote

SANCTIFICATION: THE EXPERIENCE AND THE ETHICS
(Kansas City, Mo.: Nazarene Publishing House,
1928 - recently reprinted in paper by Schmul).
General Superintendent James B. Chapman's THE
TERMINOLOGY OF HOLINESS (Kansas City, Mo.: Beacon
Hill, 1947 - recently reissued in paperback) has
had wide circulation. A strict view of holiness
doctrine is defended in Stephen S. White, ERADICA-
TION DEFINED, EXPLAINED, AUTHENTICATED (Kansas
City, Mo.: Beacon Hill, 1954 - reissued in paperback). W.T. Purkiser has written two popular
short treatments, CONFLICTING CONCEPTS OF HOLINESS
(Kansas City, Mo.: Beacon Hill, 1953) and SANCTI-
FICATION AND ITS SYNONYMS (Kansas City, Mo.:
Beacon Hill, 1961 - recently reissued in paperback).
These two books are helpful in gaining insight into
contemporary debate. The most outstanding holiness theologian today is no doubt Richard Taylor
of the Nazarene Seminary. His is a somewhat updated, but traditional approach. His most important works are A RIGHT CONCEPTION OF SIN (Kansas
City, Missouri: Nazarene Publishing House, 1939 -
recently reissued in paper), THE DISCIPLINED LIFE
(Kansas City, Mo.: Beacon Hill, 1962 - available
in paper), and LIFE IN THE SPIRIT (Kansas City,
Mo.: Beacon Hill, 1966 - available also in
paper).[26]

---

26. Much literature has of course risen to attack
    the holiness theology. One of the earliest
of these on the American scene was Samuel Franklin's
A CRITICAL REVIEW OF WESLEYAN PERFECTION (Cincin-
nati: Methodist Book Concern, 1866). Also within
Methodism, but arising out of the controversies
just before the turn of the century were J.M.
Boland, THE PROBLEM OF METHODISM (Nashville:
Printed for the Author by the Publishing House of
the Methodist Episcopal Church, South, 1888) and
James Mudge, GROWTH IN HOLINESS TOWARD PERFECTION,

Periodicals

By its very nature, the Holiness Movement has found major expression in periodical literature. This material is just beginning to be studied. Delbert Rose of Asbury has published a list of over 60 holiness periodicals (mostly discontinued) as Appendix C (pp. 273-4) of his THEOLOGY OF CHRISTIAN EXPERIENCE. Appendix C2 (pp. 437-450) of Charles Jones, "Perfectionist Persuasion" nearly triples this figure and provides founding dates, title changes, sponsorship, and cross references from variant titles. Dr. Rose is continuing his compilations and has added information to both lists, but nothing is ready yet for further publication.

Perhaps most important was the GUIDE TO CHRISTIAN PERFECTION founded in Boston in 1839. In 1845 the title became GUIDE TO HOLINESS. It was purchased by Dr. W.C. Palmer and moved to New York City where it was published until 1901. Phoebe Palmer took over the editing and by 1873 circulation had reached 40,000.

OR PROGRESSIVE SANCTIFICATION (New York: Hunt and Eaton, 1895) among others. H.A. Ironside, who had unfortunate experiences with the Salvation Army, launched a fierce attack in HOLINESS: THE FALSE AND THE TRUE (New York: Loiseaux Brothers, 1912) which went through ten printings in the next 30 years. We have already mentioned Benjamin B. Warfield's PERFECTIONISM which treats most of the related movements, but does not directly attack Wesleyan perfectionism. Finally, a short article by C.T. Craig should be mentioned, "Paradox of Holiness: New Testament Doctrine of Sanctification," INTERPRETATION, VI (April, 1952), 147-61. This article attacks the Biblical foundations of the doctrine.

Out of the National Camp Meeting Association came
in 1876 the CHRISTIAN STANDARD (first published as
the METHODIST HOME JOURNAL) and in 1870 the CHRIS-
TIAN WITNESS (originally the ADVOCATE OF CHRISTIAN
HOLINESS) which ceased publication finally in 1959.
The CHRISTIAN WITNESS is presently being collated
for filming by the ATLA Board of Microtext. From
1948-1957 the STANDARD OF HOLINESS served as the
organ of the NHA and ceased publication so as not
to compete with denominational organs.

Before the turn of the century a number of region-
al holiness association published periodicals.
Among these were the BANNER OF HOLINESS (Western
Holiness Association), THE HIGHWAY (Iowa Holiness
Association), THE GOOD WAY (Southwestern Holiness
Association), MICHIGAN HOLINESS RECORD (Michigan
Holiness Association) and the PACIFIC HERALD OF
HOLINESS (Pacific Coast Holiness Association), etc.

Holiness periodicals also grew up around major
figures and schools. Associated with Martin Wells
Knapp and God's Bible School in Cincinnati was
GOD'S REVIVALIST AND BIBLE ADVOCATE (1888 - date,
before the turn of the century as THE REVIVALIST).
Associated with the Chicago Evangelistic Institute
(now Vennard College of Iowa) was HEART AND LIFE
which was founded in 1911 and ceased publication
in the 1950's. Associated with Henry Clay
Morrison and now with Asbury Theological Seminary
has been the HERALD (published under a variety of
titles but especially the PENTECOSTAL HERALD),
1888 - date.

Several denominational papers have long histories.
The WESLEYAN ADVOCATE dates back through the
WESLEYAN METHODIST to the TRUE WESLEYAN founded in
1843. The FREE METHODIST, recently retitled LIGHT
AND LIFE, dates from 1868. THE GOSPEL TRUMPET,
retitled VITAL CHRISTIANITY in 1963, has served as
the organ of the Church of God (Anderson, Indiana)

since 1881. The NAZARENE MESSENGER (founded in 1896) became the HERALD OF HOLINESS in 1912. The latter title is being collated for filming by the ATLA Board of Microtext. Other denominational periodicals can be located in the standard sources or with the help of the Jones dissertation, "Perfectionist Persuasion."

Other periodicals have arisen more recently. Since 1941 we have had the AMERICAN HOLINESS JOURNAL published by the West Publishing Company of Apollo, Pa. More recently we have had the CONVENTION HERALD published by H.E. Schmul of Salem, Ohio as the organ of the Interdenominational Holiness Convention, the umbrella organization for several of the very small splinter groups that have broken off from the various holiness churches.

Missions

The Holiness Movement has from the beginning had a strong missionary orientation, perhaps because it arose during the great century of missions and perhaps because of the influence of Acts 1:8 which conjoins the power of the Holy Spirit with witnessing to the end of the earth. Most denominations have their own board and missions program. The work of the Nazarenes has been described in a three volume work by Mendell Taylor, FIFTY YEARS OF NAZARENE MISSIONS (Kansas City, Mo.: Beacon Hill, 1952-1958). For the Pilgrims, innumerable small works describe specific fields, but the major survey is by Paul William Thomas, "An Historical Survey of Pilgrim World Missions." (Unpublished B.D. thesis, Asbury Theological Seminary, 1963). Byron S. Lamson has chronicled the work of the Free Methodists in VENTURE! THE FRONTIERS OF FREE METHODISM (Winona Lake, Ind.: Light and Life Press, 1960). Other material is described on pages 556-580 of Jones "Perfectionist

Persuasion" under the heading of the appropriate group. Current material usually may be found either in the denominational organ, or its missions magazine where that exists.

Two interdenominational mission boards have been associated with the holiness movement as a whole. Both date from the turn of the century. The first of these is the Oriental Mission Society founded in 1901 by Mr. and Mrs. Charles Cowman. Mrs. Lettie Burd Cowman is well known as the author of the widely read STREAMS IN THE DESERT, a devotional book. She also wrote a biography of her husband, CHARLES E. COWMAN, MISSIONARY WARRIOR (Los Angeles: Oriental Missionary Society, 1928) which serves as a major source for the early history of the OMS. There is also a biography of Mrs. Cowman by Benjamin H. Pearson, THE VISION LIVES (Los Angeles: Cowman Publications, 1961). More recently Edward and Esther Erny have written NO GUARANTEE BUT GOD: THE STORY OF THE FOUNDERS OF THE ORIENTAL MISSION- ARY SOCIETY (Greenwood, Ind.: Oriental Missionary Society, 1969). Current material is available in the ORIENTAL MISSIONARY STANDARD, organ of the OMS since 1901. OMS work is concentrated in South America as well as the Orient.

45

The second of these interdenominational boards, the National Holiness Missionary Society, was founded in 1910. The story of this organization was chronicled by W.W. Cary, STORY OF THE NATIONAL HOLINESS MISSIONARY SOCIETY (Chicago: National Holiness Missionary Society, 1940). Laura Cammack Trachsel picks up this story, now under the name World Gospel Mission, in three works, KINDLED FIRES IN AFRICA, KINDLED FIRES IN ASIA, and KINDLED FIRES IN LATIN AMERICA (Marion, Ind.: World Gospel Mission, 1960-1). Current material is available in CALL TO PRAYER, the organ of WGM since 1919.

Perhaps the term is too exalted, for although the
holiness movement has always drawn on the hymnody
of the whole church and especially the Wesleys,
the "gospel song" of the camp meeting is perhaps
most characteristic of the movement as a whole.
The impress of the camp meeting is still very much
felt. As nearly as I can determine this material
is to date little studied. The treatments that
are available deal with the camp meetings early in
the 19th century before the holiness revival or with
Ira Sankey of the Moody Revivals before the turn
of the next century. Some preliminary treatment
is found in Jones, "Perfectionist Persuasion."

Amazing numbers of gospel song hymnals for the use
of the holiness camp meetings were published during
the 19th century. Delbert Rose of Asbury maintains
a collection of several shelves for the CHA historical collection. A number of these were issued
under the auspices of the National Camp Meeting
Association. Among these are such titles as John
Inskip, SONGS OF TRIUMPH, ADAPTED TO PRAYER MEET-
INGS, CAMP MEETINGS AND ALL OTHER SEASONS OF
RELIGIOUS WORSHIP (Philadelphia: National Pub-
lishing Assn. for the Promotion of Holiness, 1882)
and William McDonald and Lewis Hortsough, BEULAH
SONGS: A CHOICE COLLECTION OF POPULAR HYMNS AND
MUSIC, NEW AND OLD, ESPECIALLY ADAPTED TO CAMP
MEETINGS, PRAYER AND CONFERENCE MEETINGS, FAMILY
WORSHIP AND ALL OTHER ASSEMBLIES WHERE JESUS IS
PRAISED (Philadelphia: National Association for
the Promotion of Holiness, 1879). Similar is
William McDonald, et al., SONGS OF JOY AND GLADNESS
(Boston: McDonald & Gill, 1885) and Joshua Bill
and George A. McLaughlin, GOOD NEWS IN SONG
(Boston: The Christian Witness Co., 1891). As
late as 1953, a similar title was published for
the use of the "Interdenominational Holiness
Movement" with an endorsement of the NHA Executive

Secretary, Dr. H.M. Couchenour. This was Kenneth
H. Wells, SONGS OF GRACE AND POWER (Chicago:
Evangel Mission Company, 1953).

The Nazarene Church perhaps has its roots most
directly in this tradition. Of particular significance for them has been Haldor Lillenas, a con-
verted immigrant, who became a pastor and music
evangelist and established a music publishing
house that had great impact in the denomination.
His autobiography is available as DOWN MELODY LANE
(Kansas City, Mo.: Beacon Hill, 1953), and much
of his work can be found in the Nazarene hymnal,
PRAISE AND WORSHIP (Kansas City, Mo.: Lillenas
Pub. Co., n.d.), now being revised.

Most of the denominations now have their own
hymnals, often differing little from those of
larger denominations. One of the finest is a
joint effort by the Wesleyans and the Free Methodists, HYMNS OF THE LIVING FAITH (Marion, Ind.:
Wesleyan Methodist Publishing Assn., 1951 and
Winona Lake, Ind.: Light and Life Press, 1951),
now being revised, again by a joint committee.
Here one will find hymns by Phoebe Palmer, Haldor
Lillenas, and Ira Sankey with the finest efforts
of the whole Christian church.

Preaching

Much of the material cited above under "theology"
actually consisted originally of sermons and
addresses in churches or camp meetings. In addition certain collections of sermons have been compiled that can serve as illustrations of the
homiletical art of the holiness preachers. Again
available, though in mutilated form, is THE DOUBLE
CURE, OR ECHOES FROM NATIONAL CAMP MEETINGS
(Boston: McDonald and Gill, 1887 - the first 206
pages have been reprinted in paperback by Schmul,

1965). From the turn of the century we have THE
PENTECOSTAL PULPIT (Louisville: Pentecostal Pub-
lishing Co., n.d.) and TWENTIETH CENTURY HOLINESS
SERMONS (Louisville: Pentecostal Publishing Co., -
I have seen four printings and none carry a date).

In the twentieth century the Nazarenes have produced several items. First of these was THE
NAZARENE PULPIT (Kansas City, Mo.: Nazarene Publishing House, 1925), which contains thumbnail
sketches and photos of the preachers included.
More recently have appeared D. Shelby Corlett
(ed.), THE SECOND WORK OF GRACE (Kansas City, Mo.:
Beacon Hill, 1950) and James McGraw (ed.), THE
HOLINESS PULPIT (Kansas City, Mo.: Beacon Hill,
1957.) Theologian Richard S. Taylor devoted his
most recent book to the topic PREACHING HOLINESS
TODAY (Kansas City, Mo.: Beacon Hill, 1968) which
originated in preaching seminars held at the NHA
annual conventions and is apparently designed for
his classes at the Nazarene Seminary. His bibliography (pp. 206-210) includes a list of holiness
sermons. Probably the most outstanding holiness
preacher today is Paul S. Rees, son of Seth Rees
and for years pastor of the First Covenant Church
of Minneapolis. From this period date THE FACT OF
OUR LORD (Grand Rapids: Eerdmans, 1951) and IF
GOD BE FOR US! (Grand Rapids: Eerdmans, 1940),
both of which went through several printings. More
recent books have consisted more of addresses or
biblical expositions.

I am aware of two magazines designed for preachers
within the holiness movement. For ten years (1949-
1958) W.C. Mavis of Asbury Seminary edited the
CHRISTIAN MINISTER, designed primarily for Free
Methodists. Still being published among the
Nazarenes (and founded in 1926) is the NAZARENE
PREACHER (Originally the PREACHER'S MAGAZINE).
The latter is more helpful, including among other
things theological articles and treatments of

various preachers important to the holiness tradition.

Historical Collections

Since I have done little archival work myself, I am here relying on the reports of those who have. For the 19th century one must turn primarily to the Methodist sources - the schools, the archives at the Methodist Historical Society at Lake Junaluska, N.C., and the Methodist Publishing House in Nashville. I am told that Drew's collection is particularly good in this area and what spot-checking I was able to do seems to confirm this. No doubt the UNION LIST OF METHODIST SERIALS and the METHODIST UNION CATALOG will be of great help in locating this material once they are published. The preliminary and checking editions serve somewhat in the meantime. Asbury has joined both of these and will list her collection there.

The archives and historical collection of the Christian Holiness Association are now in the hands of the official historian Dr. Delbert Rose of Asbury Seminary and are stored for the present in the B.L. Fisher Library. Dr. Rose is currently producing from this material a history of the Association. His personal files also contain a great deal of interest. Asbury Theological Seminary has of course a significant collection, including files of the PENTECOSTAL HERALD, an index to Henry Clay Morrison's work therein, and an unorganized collection of the imprints of the Pentecostal Publishing Co. of Louisville. There are unfortunately many gaps.

As one moves out of the 19th century one must turn to the institutions or schools that have been produced by various facets of the movement. God's Bible School of Cincinnati has been associated with important figures, publishing and churches within the movement. Mention should perhaps also be made of Vennard College near Oskaloosa, Iowa (formerly the Chicago Evangelistic Institute) which is providing much of the CHRISTIAN WITNESS for ATLA filming.

Among the denominations, the Nazarenes have been perhaps the most assiduous. In 1955 they established a "Church History Commission" to collect the historical materials relating to the Nazarenes and to commission CALLED UNTO HOLINESS by Timothy Smith. He comments that nearly all the materials behind his book have been collected in Kansas City in the original or on microfilm. H.V. Synan comments in his dissertation, "The Pentecostal Movement in the United States," that this collection "constitutes the best source for manuscripts, periodicals, and general accounts relating to the National Holiness Movement and the holiness denominations which issued from it" (p. 277). I also understand that the collection at Pasadena College is particularly good and that Eastern Nazarene College has recently embarked on the development of a "holiness library" to collect at least the relevant books.

Most other holiness denominations have made some efforts to collect some materials. Bishop Leslie Marston has been engaged in this task for the Free Methodists. Some work has been done for the Wesleyans. The materials for the Church of God (Anderson, Ind.) have been collected in the Warner Memorial Collection of the School of Theology of Anderson College, Anderson, Indiana.

Recent Trends

Perhaps some recent trends and related bibliography would be of interest. I have held back some items that could have been mentioned earlier for treatment here.

1. Born in the forces of revivalism, the Holiness
    Movement still expects and sees God's power
manifested in the "revival." This has been particularly true of Asbury College where over the
past twenty-five years there have been a number of
"spontaneous revivals." The manifestations of
1950 and 1958 were chronicled in a booklet by
Henry C. James and Paul Rader, HALLS AFLAME
(Wilmore, Ky.: Asbury Seminary Press, 1959). A
much larger book tells the story of the events of
the first week of February, 1970, and their impact
on a wide number of colleges, churches and institutions, mostly within the holiness movement. The
volume was edited by Robert E. Coleman of Asbury
Theological Seminary as ONE DIVINE MOMENT (Old
Tappan, N.J.: Revell, 1970). Another contributor,
Henry C. James, has maintained at Asbury Seminary
a file of newspaper clippings, etc. associated
with these events.

2. The holiness movement remains firmly evange-
    listic in nature. While most denominations
are decreasing in membership, most holiness denominations are still vigorously growing. There
is also a department of evangelism at Asbury
Theological Seminary. The S.E. McCreless Chair of
Evangelism is occupied by Robert E. Coleman who
studied "Factors in the Expansion of the Methodist
Episcopal Church from 1784 to 1812" (unpublished
doctoral dissertation, University of Iowa, 1954)
and applies his discoveries in such works as THE
MASTER PLAN OF EVANGELISM (Westwood, N.J.: Revell,
1964) , already translated into several languages,
and DRY BONES CAN LIVE AGAIN: REVIVAL IN THE
LOCAL CHURCH (Old Tappan, N.J.: Revell, 1969).
The Nazarenes have produced a major work in this
area by Mendell Taylor, EXPLORING EVANGELISM
(Kansas City, Mo.: Beacon Hill, 1964).

3. The social concern of the original Wesleyan
Revival and the mid-19th century revivals is
being recovered (not least because of pressure of
the younger generation!). A department of church
and society has been established at Asbury Theological Seminary, and Gilbert James of that department has been the motivating force behind a new
"Urban Ministry Program for Seminarians" (UMPS) in
Chicago sponsored by a number of co-operating
seminaries and funded by the Lilly Foundation.
This concern has so far not produced any literature
other than a few essays in NHA collections about
to be mentioned.

4. Although denominations within the holiness
movement consistently ignore the conciliar
movements on the national and international level,
they are fiercely ecumenical within their own
circle. In 1966, some consideration was given to
turning the NHA into a federation of holiness
churches. In the last very few years mergers have
produced both the Missionary Church and the
Wesleyan Church. In its merging conference, the
Wesleyan Church voted to initiate discussions with
the Free Methodists. These movements have been
studied by Howard A. Snyder, "Unity and the Holiness Churches" (B.D. thesis, Asbury Theological
Seminary, 1966).

5. Unfortunately the pattern of schism is just as
firmly embedded in the tradition. Mergers and
other forces have resulted in the formation of a
number of very small, conservative holiness denominations. These include such groups as the
Allegheny Wesleyan Methodist Connection, the Bible
Missionary Church (originally Nazarene), the
Wesleyan Holiness Association (originally Bible
Missionary Church), the United Holiness Church and
the Evangelical Wesleyan Church (both originally
Free Methodist). These groups are loosely grouped
today in the Inter-Denominational Holiness

Convention, which announced that 22 groups were participating in its 1971 Convention. This group is also now sponsoring a seminary of sorts, Aldersgate School of Religion, Hobe Sound, Florida. The IHC is being studied by David Webb of Asbury Seminary in a Th.M. thesis.

6. The 1960's have seen a renewed emphasis on scholarship. There has been founded a Wesleyan Theological Society that issues the WESLEYAN THEOLOGICAL JOURNAL now in its 6th volume (Spring, 1971), which publishes the papers of the annual November meetings. This joins the ASBURY SEMINARIAN (founded 1946), the only other theological journal in the movement. In the early 1960's the NHA sponsored a number of "doctrinal seminars" in which scholars within the movement read papers in the various educational institutions. These were collected by the president Kenneth Geiger, the motivating force behind the seminars, into three anthologies, INSIGHTS INTO HOLINESS (Kansas City, Mo.: Beacon Hill, 1962), FURTHER INSIGHTS INTO HOLINESS (Kansas City, Mo.: Beacon Hill, 1963), and THE WORD AND THE DOCTRINE (Kansas City, Mo.: Beacon Hill, 1965). Papers and addresses of the 1968 centennial convention of the NHA were collected as PROJECTING OUR HERITAGE (Kansas City, Mo.: Beacon Hill, 1969) edited by Myron F. Boyd and Merne A. Harris.

53

7. For the most part holiness theology has remained unaffected by 20th century theological currents and turmoil. Some have suggested that in its harking back to Arminius as its theological forefather it might provide balancing emphases to some of the more extreme positions of modern neo-Reformation theology (cf. Carl Bangs, "Recent Studies in Arminianism," RELIGION IN LIFE, XXXII [Summer, 1963], p. 421). But so far no one has taken up the task of demonstrating this. Some within the tradition have been so bold as to

notice certain affinities within the movement to at least some forms of existentialism (see, for example, certain articles in the Spring-Summer, 1957 issue of the ASBURY SEMINARIAN). One of these, Nazarene theologian Mildred Bangs Wynkoop, is seeing through the press what promises to be a strikingly new interpretation of the Wesleyan message, LOVE - THE DYNAMIC OF WESLEYANISM (to be published in 1972 by Beacon Hill Press). A section of this appeared in the 1971 WESLEYAN THEOLOGICAL JOURNAL. The present writer has been investigating certain affinities between Wesley's SERMONS and Sören Kiekegaard's STAGES ON LIFE'S WAY.

8. But recent historical studies of the sources of the movement have been manifold. Many of these have already been mentioned in the course of the paper. One of the finest of these is by Free Methodist George Turner of Asbury and is based on his Harvard dissertation (1946). This was published first as THE MORE EXCELLENT WAY (Winona Lake: Light and Life Press, 1952) and has recently been made available with some revision as THE VISION WHICH TRANSFORMS (Kansas City, Mo.: Beacon Hill, 1964 - reprinted 1970). This volume treats the biblical basis for perfection and traces the concept through the whole history of the church until the present day. Others start with Arminius in finding theological foundations. Nazarene Mildred Wynkoop has written FOUNDATIONS OF WESLEYAN-ARMINIAN THEOLOGY (Kansas City, Mo.: Beacon Hill, 1967) and her brother Carl Bangs, formerly a Nazarene and now a Methodist teaching at St. Paul School of Theology, studied Arminius in his University of Chicago doctoral program. Out of this has come ARMINIUS: A STUDY IN THE DUTCH REFORMATION to be published in June, 1971, by Abingdon. Most writers start however with the Wesleyan revival. One of the finest interpretations of this period has been by Free Methodist Mary Alice Tenney of Greenville College, BLUEPRINT

FOR A CHRISTIAN WORLD (Winona Lake: Light and
Life Press, 1953). Wesleyan Leo Cox has contributed JOHN WESLEY'S CONCEPT OF PERFECTION (Kansas
City, Mo.: Beacon Hill, 1964) based on his Iowa
dissertation (1959). We have already mentioned
the efforts to tell the story of the American
movement. A number of other such studies exist as
dissertations but have not been published, and
others are in process.

9. There has been a striking increase in biblical
   studies within the last few years. Two multi-
volume Bible commentaries have been produced. The
Nazarenes produced the 10 volume BEACON BIBLE
COMMENTARY (Kansas City, Mo.: Beacon Hill, 1964-
69). A similar project, drawing on many of the
same writers, has been edited by Charles W. Carter
of Taylor University, the WESLEYAN BIBLE COMMENTARY
(Grand Rapids: Eerdmans, 1964-69), six volumes in
7 parts (volume I having two sections). Dr.
George Turner of Asbury Seminary attempted to draw
on a larger community to produce an EVANGELICAL
BIBLE COMMENTARY, modeled after the INTERPRETER'S
BIBLE. This project collapsed after the appearance of the other two series, but nearly all the
volumes produced were by holiness writers.[27] The

---

27. Directly in the series were Ralph Earle, THE
    GOSPEL ACCORDING TO MARK (Grand Rapids:
Zondervan, 1957), Charles W. Carter and Ralph
Earle, THE ACTS OF THE APOSTLES (Grand Rapids:
Zondervan, 1959), George A. Turner and Julius R.
Mantey, THE GOSPEL ACCORDING TO JOHN (Grand Rapids:
Eerdmans, 1964). Intended for inclusion, but
since published separately was the contribution of
British Methodist C. Leslie Mitton, THE EPISTLE OF
JAMES (Grand Rapids: Eerdmans, 1966). Other
books, such as Turner on Hebrews, exist in manu-
script and may yet see light in another form.

holiness schools have tended to perpetuate a
school of biblical interpretation called "Inductive
Bible Study" or "English Bible" developed primarily
at Biblical Seminary in New York City after the
turn of the century. The major text of this
approach is by Asbury Seminary's Dean Robert A.
Traina, formerly of Biblical, METHODICAL BIBLE
STUDY (latest printing available from the author,
Wilmore, Ky.). This approach was developed for
lay use in the Sunday Schools by Donald Joy (exec.
editor), ALDERSGATE BIBLICAL SERIES (published by
Light and Life Press of the Free Methodist Church).
The set of 40 volumes is still available and has
been used by a number of the holiness denominations, especially the Wesleyans and the Free
Methodists.

10. Finally, the movement has been influenced by
      the rise of psychology. Particular challen-
ges were raised by this area of study for a movement which has so emphasized Christian experience.
These men arose particularly among the Free Methodists. Bishop Leslie Marston made signal contributions in the field of psychology before turning
more to church work and the history of the denomination. He has also written FROM CHAOS TO CHARAC-
TER: A STUDY IN THE STEWARDSHIP OF PERSONALITY
(3rd ed., Winona Lake, Ind.: Light and Life Press,
1944). Orville S. Walters of the University of
Illinois has made contributions primarily in
journals in the field of psychiatry and also in
such publications as RELIGION IN LIFE. W. Curry
Mavis of Asbury Seminary has also produced several
books, most important of which has been the
PSYCHOLOGY OF CHRISTIAN EXPERIENCE (Grand Rapids:
Zondervan, 1963 - recently reissued in paperback).
The impact of such thinking has been to shift the
approach to Christian experience away from the
dogmatic patterns of the past to a more open,
need-oriented pattern of pastoral ministry.

THE AMERICAN PENTECOSTAL MOVEMENT

A Bibliographical Essay

57

THE AMERICAN PENTECOSTAL MOVEMENT

A BIBLIOGRAPHICAL ESSAY

by

David W. Faupel

The Second in a Series of
"Occasional Bibliographic Papers
of the B. L. Fisher Library"

B. L. Fisher Library
Asbury Theological Seminary
Wilmore, Kentucky 40390
1972

This Essay is a Revised Version
of the Text Published Originally in
the 1972 PROCEEDINGS of the
American Theological Library Association

Price

1 - 10 copies $3.00 ea.
11 or more $2.50 ea.

plus postage and handling
unless payment accompanies order.

Copies may be ordered from:

David W. Faupel
B. L. Fisher Library
Asbury Theological Seminary
Wilmore, Kentucky 40390

This project was deemed appropriate to follow Donald Dayton's The American Holiness Movement: A Bibliographic Introduction, which was the first publication in the B. L. Fisher Library bibliographic series. A summary of this essay on Pentecostalism was presented to the twenty-sixth annual conference of the American Theological Library Association held at Waterloo, Ontario, in June 1972. This is a revised text of the essay as it appears in the 1972 Proceedings of the Association.

When leaders of the Society for Pentecostal Studies learned of the proposed project, they expressed interest in this effort to gain bibliographic control of the extensive literature in the Pentecostal Movement. As a result this paper is published as the Second Occasional Paper in the B. L. Fisher Library Bibliographic Series and as the first publication of the Society for Pentecostal Studies.

I wish to express appreciation to Peter VandenBerge, then vice-president of ATLA, for providing a place on the program for the paper and to the Association for granting permission to print the paper as a monograph.

61

I am indebted to several colleagues on the faculty of Asbury Theological Seminary: Delbert R. Rose, Professor of Biblical Theology and Historian for the Christain Holiness Association; Kenneth C. Kinghorn, Professor of Church History; Robert A. Traina, Academic Dean; Miss Susan A. Schultz, Director of Library Services; and Donald W. Dayton, former Acquisitions Librarian, for their encouragement and critical evaluation of the manuscript.

I am also grateful to Vinson Synan, secretary of SPS and William Menzies, former president of SPS for their guidance and encouragement in the initial stages of the project. In addition, they, along with Zenas Bicket, Donald Bowdle, Steven Durasoff, William MacDonald, and Russell Spittler, all members of SPS, read the manuscript, providing many helpful suggestions and corrections. Oral Roberts University graciously made its Pentecostal Collection available to me, and Mrs. Juanita Raudszus, ORU's Learning Resources Librarian, provided several bibliographic tools which saved many hours of labor.

Finally, I wish to express my thanks to several mem-

bers of the B. L. Fisher Library staff: Len Chester
typed the first draft from a difficult manuscript;
Mrs. Esther Richter prepared the final copy for
printing; and David Bundy and Mrs. Esther James did
much of the editing and proofreading.

The literature mentioned in this paper is scattered
throughout the United States; therefore, checking all
data for bibliographical accuracy proved to be a problem. I accept full responsibility for any errors
which may appear, and would greatly appreciate re-
ceiving information on any inaccuracy discovered by
the readers.

David W. Faupel
Public Services Librarian
    and Instructor in Biblio-
    graphy and Research
B. L. Fisher Library
Asbury Theological Seminary

62

CONTENTS

63

INTRODUCTION

In presenting a bibliographical introduction to the Pentecostal Movement several decisions had to be made.

First there is the problem of definition. William Menzies, in his work <u>Anointed to Serve: the Story of the Assemblies of God</u> (Springfield, Mo.: Gospel Publishing House, 1971), writes:

> The Pentecostal Movement is that group of sects within the Christian Church which is characterized by the belief that the occurrence mentioned in Acts 2 on the Day of Pentecost not only signaled the birth of the church, but described an experience available to believers in all ages. The experience of an enduement with power, called the "baptism in the Holy Spirit" is believed to be evidenced by the accompanying sign of "speaking with other tongues as the Spirit gives utterance" (p. 9).

Menzies suggests such a definition is inadequate to measure the complete spread of the Pentecostal Movement. Two recent developments must be noted. First the "Pentecostal experience" has spread to the historic churches, both Catholic and Protestant. To date no one has been able to measure accurately its growth and influence. However, this phase of the Pentecostal Movement has produced a great deal of literature which must be noted to make this essay complete. A second development is the "Jesus Movement." Those associated with this movement stand largely outside of organized Christianity, though many hold to the Pentecostal doctrinal distinctive. These two trends are noted in this essay, but emphasis is placed on the literature of those groups which fall within the bounds of the definition cited.

The Pentecostal Movement became international almost immediately. This essay makes little attempt to trace the literature outside the United States, except in those cases that have a direct bearing on the American scene.

A final point of discussion before beginning the
writing of the essay is stating criteria for organization of the literature.

The majority of scholarly works on the Pentecostal
Movement are written from an historical perspective.
I have been influenced by these works in my general
approach to the literature——grouping the material
around major trends and controversies as they appear
historically within the Movement. I feel that such
an approach does the most justice to the literature,
enables the reader to gain a better understanding
of the Movement, and points out quickly the gaps
that need further research.

WORLD-WIDE SURVEYS

The starting point for understanding the Pentecostal
Movement is John Thomas Nichol, Pentecostalism (New
York: Harper and Row, 1966). It has been reissued
in paperback by the Logos Press of Plainfield, New
Jersey, with a new title, The Pentecostals. This
work, originally a Ph.D. dissertation at Boston
University, gives a bird's-eye view of the growth
of Pentecostalism on the world scene.

Nichol's major contribution to existing literature
is that he has shown the rise of the Pentecostal
Movement internationally in relation to its American origins.

The chief weakness of the book is his treatment of
individual denominations in the Pentecostal Movement. He groups them by size rather than by their
organizational structure or doctrinal emphasis.
His approach shows little understanding for the factors leading to the existence of so many Pentecostal denominations.1

---

1. E. L. Moore in an M.A. thesis, "A Handbook of
    Pentecostal Denominations in the United States,"
lists over forty separate Pentecostal bodies. Walter J. Hollenweger, in his newly published work,
The Pentecostals: The Charismatic Movement in the
Churches, p. 29, claims to know of the existence of
at least two hundred Pentecostal bodies in the
United States. (Many are no larger than a handful
of churches.)

Though Nichol provides little new material, he has brought together the best of previous Pentecostal scholarship, and, for this reason, his book serves as an excellent introduction to the Movement. His nine-page classified bibliography is helpful for further studies.

Without doubt the most comprehensive work on Pentecostalism has been done by Walter J. Hollenweger, formerly Executive Secretary of the Department of Studies in Evangelism of the World Council of Churches. He is currently professor of mission at the University of Birmingham in England. Like Nichol, he is the son of a Pentecostal minister; he pastored a Pentecostal church himself for ten years.

His multi-volume Zurich dissertation,"Handbuch der Pfingstbewegung," ['65]available on microfilm from ATLA Board of Microtext, is a goldmine of historical, doctrinal, and statistical information on Pentecostal groups throughout the world.

Hollenweger's work is difficult to assess. The size and scope of his work is staggering. However, one gains the distinct impression that his analysis rests as much on his presuppositions as on the data he has collected. The work must be a starting point for all future research.

Hollenweger has summarized his work in Enthusiastisches Christentum: die Pfingstbewegung in Geschichte und Gegenwart (Zurich: Rolf Brockhaus Wuppental, 1966). This was recently translated into English as The Pentecostals: the Charismatic Movement in the Church (Minneapolis: Augsburg, 1972). Especially helpful are his notes at the end of each chapter and a thirty-five page annotated bibliography.

A third work on International Pentecostalism is Nils Bloch-Hoell, The Pentecostal Movement; its Origin, Development and Distinctive Character (Oslo: Universitetsforlaget; London: Allen and Unwin; and New York: Humanities Press, 1964). This work, a revised English translation of a 1956 Norwegian work Pinsebevegelsen, is currently the most comprehensive work on Pentecostalism in Europe that has been published in English. The author's analysis, especially of American Pentecostal doctrine and distinctives, reflects his European background.

Major concern has been expressed by some American

Pentecostal scholars concerning Bloch-Hoell's understanding of the origin and development of Pentecostalism in the U. S. However, Walter Hollenweger
has stated that his description of the Azusa Street
Revival is the most extensive and accurate to date.[2]

Bloch-Hoell concludes his work with fifty-five pages
of bibliographical notes that are most helpful in
giving additional detail that is not normally located elsewhere. His bibliography contains mainly
non-English items which are not listed in most bibliographies on Pentecostalism.

CLASSIFICATION OF AMERICAN PENTECOSTAL GROUPS

Everett L. Moore, "Handbook of Pentecostal Denominations in the United States" (Pasadena: Pasadena
College, June 1954), an unpublished M.A. thesis,
must be first considered.[3]

Moore's work claims no profundity, but does render a
practical service by listing forty Pentecostal denominations, organized around the following categories:

1. Those denominations which hold a Keswick
   view of sanctification.
2. Those denominations which hold a Holiness
   view of "entire sanctification."
3. Those denominations which hold a "Jesus
   Only" view of the God-head.

----

2. Walter S. Hollenweger, "A Black Pentecostal Concept; A Forgotten Chapter in Black History,"
Concept, Special Issue 30, June 1970, Papers from
the Department on Studies in Evangelism, World Council of Churches, p. 14.

3. Because Moore's "Handbook" makes this analysis,
   in addition to its obvious use as a reference
tool, serious consideration should be given to update this work and make it available in published
form. It also serves to remind us that the time
has come for the Pentecostal bodies, as listed in
Frank S. Mead, Handbook of Denominations in the
United States (Nashville: Abingdon Press, 1970, 5th
ed.) and the Yearbook of American Churches, to be
reorganized along the lines suggested by Moore.

He concludes with a brief appendix on the Latter
Rain Movement.

For each denomination he gives a brief historical
sketch, its doctrinal statement and ecclesiastical
structure.

Moore quite rightly suggests that:

> For the first fourteen years, the Movement
> had no standard of doctrine because its mem-
> bership was drawn from various backgrounds,
> held together only by faith in speaking in
> other tongues. It was during these years
> that various groups found small nuclei from
> which later grew the numerous Pentecostal
> Churches today in existence (p. 20).

In an analysis of Moore's work, one quickly dis-
covers the several factors which led to the rise
of so many Pentecostal groups.

First were the doctrinal divisions mentioned above.
But within these theological groupings, several
other factors emerged to cause further splittings:
(1) Race: This is such an important factor that I
have elected to do a separate division of my essay
on this issue, in addition to the theological
groupings. (2) Church Government: Within each
theological grouping, congregational, presbyterian,
and episcopal forms of church polity emerged. (3)
Strong personalities: A. J. Tomlinson and Aimee
Semple McPherson are prominent examples of personalities who caused further divisions.

Klaude Kendrick, The Promise Fulfilled: A History
of the Modern Pentecostal Movement (Springfield,
Mo.: Gospel Publishing House, 1961) is also important for a study of American Pentecostalism. Kendrick is the first to group Pentecostal bodies by
the issues that were determinative in forming separate denominations.

Wesleyan Perfectionist Groups

With the appearance of Vinson Synan, The Holiness-
Pentecostal Movement in the United States (Grand
Rapids: Eerdmans, 1971), Pentecostal scholarship
has moved into a new phase of development. It
is the first analysis of the Movement seen from
the perspective of a major theological tradition

within the Movement.[4]

Synan spends a great deal of space tracing the origins of the Pentecostal Movement back through the
American Holiness Movement, Methodism, Anglicanism,
and finally to the Roman Church. Contending that
Pentecostalism arose outside the influence of Reformed theology, Synan marshalls his evidence to
support the thesis that the Pentecostal Movement in
its original form represents a division within the
Holiness Movement. Thus, in his view, those Pentecostal denominations which hold to a "finished work"
view of sanctification are seen as the first major
split in Pentecostal theology.[5]

---

4. Two other works are scheduled to be written on
    major segments within Pentecostalism: David
Reed, "Historical and Theological Origins of the
'Oneness' or 'Jesus Only' Movement"(Boston: Boston
University Ph.D. thesis topic) and Garnet Pike,
"Historical Study of Black Pentecostals" (Vander-
bilt, Ph.D. thesis topic).

5. The most extensive discussion of the issues in-
    volved regarding the doctrine of entire sancti-
fication in its Pentecostal historical context is
Irvine John Harrison's unpublished Th.D. dissertation, "A History of the Assemblies of God" (Berkeley:
Baptist Divinity School, 1954), p. 126 ff.

He notes that William H. Durham, a Baptist Englishman came to the Azusa Street Revival to teach his
doctrine of the "finished work of Christ." Harrison quotes J. Roswell Flower, an early leader of
the Assemblies of God:

> Durham carried his message to Los Angeles and
> preached it in Azusa Street...When he was
> turned out of Azusa Street, he continued his
> ministry by word of mouth and printed page in
> other quarters until his death. The emphasis
> he gave to the finished work of Christ was
> accented by ridicule of the Holiness teaching
> on sanctification as the necessary work of
> grace, and a prerequisite to the Baptism of
> the Holy Ghost. This divorced him from the
> sympathies of the Holiness groups...on the
> other hand, those of Baptistic backgrounds
> readily accepted his teaching. The contro-

Synan's strongest argument for his case is his
demonstration that early leaders in the Movement
were from the Holiness Movement and continued to
hold that position after they embraced the new
Pentecostal doctrine.

---

versy over this point of doctrine became so
acute that the Holiness groups in the South-
east, for the most part, withdrew into themselves and discouraged fellowship with the
Movement in other parts of the country (p.
132).

Two additional unpublished theses provide further
background material concerning the origins of Pentecostalism: Calvin Carmen, "The Posture of Pentecostalism in View of the Crucial Issues of the
Fundamentalist--Neo-Evangelical Debate" (Springfield, Mo.: Central Bible Institute, M.A. thesis,
1965), and Frank C. Masserano, "A Study of Worship Forms in the Assemblies of God" (Princeton,
N. J.: Princeton Theological Seminary, M.Th. thesis,
1966).

Masserano contends that while the Holiness Movement
played a large part in the rise of Pentecostalism,
the Movement must be viewed as having broader origins. He writes:

While the Pentecostal Holiness Church established a doctrine of three blessings (i.e.,
salvation, sanctification, and the Holy Spirit
Baptism), for most Pentecostals, the sanctification terminology and concepts were trans-
ferred to a Keswick interpretation of the
Holy Spirit Baptism...(p. 44)...the Keswick
doctrine of the baptism of the Holy Spirit as
taught by D. L. Moody, R. A. Torrey, and A. B.
Simpson was to be combined with the Holiness
emphasis on sanctification and enthusiasm in
defining of Pentecostal doctrine (p. 45).

In addition to these factors, Pentecostalism was
rejected outright by most Holiness groups. Also
Holiness-Pentecostal groups have been largely con-
fined to southeastern United States. (See Menzies,
Anointed to Serve, pp. 80, 81.) Synan needs to be
taken seriously. His thesis will, no doubt, be
debated among Pentecostals for years to come.

Charles F. Parham,[6] the first 20th century person
to articulate the Pentecostal doctrine that
speaking in other tongues was the initial evidence
of the baptism in the Holy Spirit, was originally a
Methodist lay minister. Synan clearly demonstrates
that Parham embraced the doctrine and received the
experience of entire sanctification. Likewise, W.
J. Seymour, a student of Parham, and the leader of
the Azusa Street Revival taught the doctrine of
entire sanctification.[7]

The evidence tends to support Synan's thesis. Pentecostal theology was developed in the context of

---

6. For a biography of this man, see Sarah E. Parham, The Life of Charles F. Parham, Founder of
the Apostolic Faith Movement (Joplin, Mo.: Tri-
State Printing Co., 1930). This apology by his
wife is obviously a highly biased account of his
life and ministry, but provides many interesting
details not found elsewhere.

7. The importance of the Azusa revival to the Pentecostal Movement cannot be over-emphasized.
Not only was it the spark that gave rise to the
Movement, but also almost all the issues which led
to the formation of the several separate denominational groups can be traced back to it. Those
issues were: (1) the dispute of the doctrine of
entire sanctification; (2) the Jesus Only, or Oneness doctrine; (3) the teaching of the Latter Rain
Covenant; and, (4) the formation of denominations
along racial lines.

For a firsthand report of the revival at Azusa
Street, one should consult Frank Bartleman, How
Pentecost Came to Los Angeles (Los Angeles: pri-
vately printed, 1928). This account has been re-
printed in an abridged form under the title, What
Really Happened at "Azusa Street" by Voice Chris-
tian Publications in 1962. It is available at
Voice magazine, Box 672, North Ridge, California.

Also an interesting autobiography of the first person to speak in tongues under Parham's ministry is
Agnes N. O. LaBerge, What God Hath Wrought--Life
and Work of Mrs. Agnes N. O. LaBerge, nee Miss
Agnes N. Ozman (Chicago: Herald Publishing Co.,
1921).

the Holiness Movement. He fails to account, however, for the other forces at work which quickly attached themselves to the Pentecostal doctrines, but rejected their holiness origins. Given this historical situation at the time, it was probably inevitable that the Movement divide over this issue. The background of too many people coming into the Pentecostal Movement at the time was too alien to the teachings of the holiness traditions. Synan also includes an excellent chapter on the black Pentecostals. I will refer to this in greater detail later.

One of the largest and oldest holiness-pentecostal churches is the Church of God (Cleveland, Tennessee). The church traces its origins back to a conference called at Barney Creek Meeting House in Monroe County, Tennessee in 1886. There Richard G. Spurling, a disenchanted Baptist, challenged the people at the conference to organize "to take the New Testament as the only rule of faith and practice, and to sit together as the Church of God to transact business."[8]

Two denominational histories document the origin and growth of this denomination. E. L. Simmons, History of the Church of God (Cleveland, Tenn.: Church of God Publishing House, 1938) is the first of these. A second, more scholarly work appeared in 1955, Charles W. Conn, Like a Mighty Army Moves the Church of God (Cleveland, Tenn.: Church of God Publishing House, 1955).

L. Howard Juillerat, Book of Minutes (Cleveland, Tenn.: Church of God Publishing House, 1922) provides invaluable resource material on the beginnings of this church.

Charles W. Conn, Pillars of Pentecost (Cleveland, Tenn.: Pathway Press, 1959) provides additional historical data through biographical sketches of the early leaders.

Additional early material may be gleaned from J. W. Buckalew, Incidents in the Life of J. W. Buckalew (Cleveland, Tenn.: Church of God Publishing House, 1920).

---

8. Kendrick, The Promise Fulfilled, p. 189.

A. J. Tomlinson, the man directly responsible for
bringing the Church of God into the Pentecostal
Movement, provides much interesting personal detail
of the early life of the church in a diary. The
diary has been edited by his son, Homer A. Tomlinson, Diary of A. J. Tomlinson, 3 Vols. (New York:
Church of God World Headquarters, 1949-1955).

Tomlinson, a Bible salesman and itinerant preacher
from Indiana, was asked to join the Church of God
in 1903. He received the Pentecostal experience in
1908 at the Church of God's annual convention under
the ministry of G. B. Cashwell, a leader of the Pentecostal Holiness Church.

For the next few years, Tomlinson enjoyed almost un-
limited authority in the Church of God until he was
impeached in 1923 for mishandling funds. He then
left the church to form the Church of God of Prophecy. For his own reaction to factors bringing
about the split, see his Answering the Call of God
(Cleveland, Tenn.: White Wing Publishing House,
n.d.).[9] Tomlinson claimed the churches which left
with him comprised the original Church of God. Only
for legal purposes was added the phrase "of Prophecy" to the name of his church.

74

Claiming the right to appoint his successor, Tomlinson designated his son, Homer, to succeed him as
General Overseer, at his death in 1943.

Thirty-four of the forty-eight state overseers approved of this move. Threatened by another church
split, Homer suggested that his younger brother
Milton, a printer by trade, be put in charge. This
move was approved by the dissenting overseers, and
Milton was ordained Bishop. One of his first official acts as Bishop was to expel his brother Homer
from the church.

Homer promptly founded the Church of God World Headquarters. Like his father before, he claimed that
he represented the Church of God that was started
in 1903 (i.e., the date his father joined the Church

---

9. E. L. Moore, "Handbook of Pentecostal Denominations," pp. 145-165, in describing the origins
of various Pentecostal bodies, provides an excellent synopsis of what followed.

of God, Cleveland, Tenn.). Homer's career has been dotted with the spectacular. He ran for President of the United States several times, and in the early sixties proclaimed himself king of the world. He tells his story in The Shout of a King (New York: The Church of God World Headquarters, 1965).

Another important denomination in this segment of the Pentecostal Movement is the Pentecostal Holiness Church.

Vinson Synan, author of The Holiness-Pentecostal Movement, is presently writing a history of the denomination. The standard history of the church to date has been Joseph E. Campbell, The Pentecostal Holiness Church 1898-1949, Its History and Background (Franklin Springs, Ga.: Publishing House of the Pentecostal Holiness Church, 1951). The work is based on a Th.D. thesis written at Union Seminary in Richmond, Virginia, in 1948.

Campbell devotes a good deal of space to the many social and theological forces which brought his church into existence. Much of this is a simple restatement of Niebuhr, Sweet, and others who have sought to explain the rise of sects on the American scene.

Campbell also places emphasis on the development of his denomination's structure. For the student interested in detailed historical background, the work will be helpful. However, little is done by way of analysis and evaluation of the significance of what has developed throughout its history. An important aspect of the book is an analytical bibliography of Pentecostal Holiness publications.

A number of biographies and autobiographies of early leaders provide added insight to the development of this church. These include: Joseph H. and Blanche L. King, Yet Speaketh; Memoirs of the Late Bishop Joseph H. King (Franklin Springs, Ga.: Publishing House of the Pentecostal Holiness Church, 1949); R. H. Lee and G. H. Montgomery, ed., Edward O. Reeves; His Life and Message (Franklin Springs, Ga.: Publishing House of the Pentecostal Holiness Church, 1940); A. E. Robinson, A Layman and the Book (Franklin Springs, Ga.: Publishing House of the Pentecostal Holiness Church, 1936); and Watson Sorrow, Some of My Experiences (Franklin Springs, Ga.: Publishing House of the Pentecostal Holiness Church, 1954). Watson Sorrow later founded The

Congregational Holiness Church. The most famous personage to emerge from the Pentecostal Holiness Church is Oral Roberts. His autobiography, The Call (New York: Doubleday and Co., 1972), relates why he left to return to the United Methodist Church.

A small denomination with historic roots back to the Azusa Street Revival is the Apostolic Faith Mission led by Florence L. Crawford. The denomination still functions in the northwest, with headquarters in Portland, Oregon. The history of the denomination is documented in A Historical Account of the Apostolic Faith, a Trinitarian Fundamental Evangelistic Organization (Portland, Ore.: Apostolic Faith Mission, 1965), and can be ordered from Apostolic Faith Publishing House, N. W. Sixth & Burnside, Portland, Oregon, 97209.

B. L. Cox, History and Doctrine of the Congregational Holiness Church (Greenwood, South Carolina: Congregational Holiness Church Publishing House, 1959) provides the basic study of this small denomination of some five thousand members which broke with the Pentecostal Holiness Church in 1920 over divine healing and church government. Cox's autobiography, My Life Story (Greenwood, South Carolina: Congregational Holiness Publishing House, 1959) gives additional information.

Luther Gibson, History of the Church of God Mountain Assembly (n.p., 1954), documents the history of the small Pentecostal denomination whose headquarters is in Jellico, Tenn. It dates back to 1906, but growth has been limited to Eastern Kentucky and Tennessee. This denomination is the only known Pentecostal group that allows its members the use of tobacco.

An extensive search failed to locate histories of the several smaller Holiness-Pentecostal denominations, for example, the Pentecostal Fire Baptized Holiness Church, Emmanuel Holiness Church, and the Fire Baptized Holiness Church of God of America.

Keswick Pentecostal Groups

To date no study has appeared that would parallel Synan's work and determine the influence of the Keswick faction on the Pentecostal Movement as a whole. The sources are so scattered that an attempt to mention them here would be beyond the limitations of this essay. The basic question to be answered in such a study is: Why did this segment of the Pentecostal Movement experience national growth from the beginning of the movement, while the gains of the Holiness tradition were contained largely to southeastern United States for almost fifty years?

Until such a study is made, one must wrestle with the contention made by Menzies that the Assemblies of God is "the most representative of the Pentecostal organizations, and can serve usefully as a microcosm of the Pentecostal Movement as a whole."[10]

The best sources for the early history of the Assemblies of God are J. Roswell Flower, "History of the Assemblies of God," a set of unpublished class notes;[11] B. F. Lawrence, The Apostolic Faith Restored (St. Louis: Gospel Publishing House, 1916); Stanley H. Frodsham, With Signs Following Rev. ed. (Springfield, Mo.: Gospel Publishing House, 1946);[12] C. C. Burnett, In the Last Days; A History of the Assemblies of God (Springfield, Mo.: Gospel Publishing House, 1962); and, Carl Brumback, Suddenly From Heaven, a History of the Assemblies of God (Springfield, Mo.: Gospel Publishing House, 1961).

Flower, more than any other single person, has stamped his image on the direction taken by the Assemblies of God. His notes are largely an apology for the Assemblies of God, designed to give second generation Pentecostals an understanding of their

---

10. Menzies, Anointed to Serve, p. 10. He further points out in a footnote that others such as Bloch-Hoell, Nichol and Kelsey (all non-Assemblies of God men) have made the same claim for the Assemblies of God. By this, he means all of the issues and forces which have been brought to bear on any part of the Pentecostal Movement have at some point affected the Assemblies of God as well. Despite initial reservations, this writer has come to accept this as basically true.

11. Copies of this are kept at Central Bible College and Evangel College in Springfield, Mo.

12. This was published originally under the title, The Pentecostal Revival, in 1941.

origins and religious heritage. Though undocumented, these notes provide an excellent opportunity to study the reflections and analysis of an eyewitness. Flower was a pioneer in attempting to tie Pentecostalism to the main stream of church history. He notes that "tongues," the distinctive teaching of the Pentecostal Movement, have made periodic appearances throughout church history, the Pentecostal Movement being the first to identify this "gift" as evidence of the baptism in the Holy Spirit.[13]

Frodsham's work is also undocumented. As a long-time editor of the Pentecostal Evangel, he was in an excellent position to note significant trends in the denomination's growth. His work provides a helpful description of mission work overseas.

Brumback's work is the most scholarly of those mentioned. His greatest contributions are biographical sketches of many of the early leaders, preserving many of their significant statements.

Without question the historian par excellence in the Assemblies of God is William W. Menzies. His latest book, Anointed to Serve, the Story of the Assemblies of God (Springfield, Mo.: Gospel Publishing House, 1971) provides us with the most recent and comprehensive history of this denomination. The book is based on his Ph.D. dissertation, "The Assemblies of God, 1941-1967: The Consolidation of a Revival Movement" (University of Iowa, 1968).

As the dissertation title implies, Menzies focuses on the last thirty years of his denomination's history. Menzies argues that the denomination has undergone two major shifts since World War II.

First, the church moved from an era of isolation to a period of interdenominational cooperation. This is seen in their association with the National Association of Evangelicals, The World Pentecostal Fellowship, and the Pentecostal Fellowship of North America. Menzies contends that this movement is in

13. Bernard L. Bresson, Studies in Ecstasy (New York: Vantage Press, 1966) catalogues twenty-four movements and sects that have appeared between the second and the nineteenth centuries which practiced the gift of speaking in tongues.

line with the intent of early Pentecostal leaders.
At the beginning the leaders did not wish to form
a new denomination; rather, they desired to remain
in the historic denominations, sharing their new
found experience with others. It was only as those
churches reacted against them that they were forced
to withdraw, form new denominations, and retreat to
isolation.

The second shift which Menzies notes is the cen-
tralization of power. Originally, the denomination
was set up to be a loose fellowship of independent
churches. Early doctrinal disputes, such as "the
new issue," set forth the trend toward centraliza-
tion. However, it was a desire for pragmatic effi-
ciency that led to the formation of a large bureau-
cracy. In recent years, a serious attempt has been
made to co-ordinate these agencies to make them more
functional.

In addition to documenting these two trends, Menzies
has provided many insights into major issues and
emphases of the denomination during these years.
The first section of his work serves as a concise
summary of the earlier histories, and like the rest
of his work, is carefully documented. Several helpful appendices, including the denomination's statement of faith, a complete historical listing of national officers and a number of statistical charts
are included. His bibliography along with those of
Synan, Brunner, and Hollenweger offer the most complete listings of Pentecostal materials.

A popularly written non-scholarly survey which should
be mentioned is Irwin Winehouse, The Assemblies of
God (New York: Vantage Press, 1959). Another excellent documented account of the organizational
structure of the Assemblies of God is Mario G.
Hoover's unpublished M.A. thesis, "Origin and Struc-
tural Development of the Assemblies of God" (Springfield, Mo.: Missouri State, 1970). Copies of this
thesis have been made available by the author and
can be purchased through the bookstore at Central
Bible College in Springfield.

An early figure in the Assemblies of God was Aimee
Semple McPherson. She soon withdrew to form her
own denomination, the International Church of the
Four Square Gospel. McPherson received an interpretation of Ezekiel's visions of the four faces--
man, lion, ox, eagle--to mean Jesus Christ; sav-

viour, baptizer, healer, and king.[14]

The history and doctrine of this denomination is compiled by Raymond L. Cox, The Four Square Gospel (Los Angeles: Heritage Committee, 1969). It can be ordered from Four Square Publications, 1100 Glendale Blvd., Los Angeles, California, 90026. Of interest are biographies of Aimee McPherson. L. Thomas, The Vanishing Evangelist; the Aimee Semple McPherson Kidnapping Affair (New York: Viking Press, 1959) offers an unfavorable analysis of her ministry. The best of the sympathetic accounts is Nancy Barr Mavity, Sister Aimee (Garden City, N. Y.: Doubleday, Duran & Co., 1931). McPherson offers several autobiographical accounts, which must also be noted: This is That: Personal Experiences, Sermons, and Writings of Aimee Semple McPherson (Los Angeles: Echo Park Evangelistic Association, 1923); In the Service of the King (New York: Boni and Liveright,, 1927); and, The Story of My Life (Los Angeles: Echo Park Evangelistic Association, 1951).

Largely due to the scandal caused by McPherson's kidnapping, several churches of her denomination in Minnesota and Iowa withdrew to form the Open Bible Evangelistic Association in 1932. This group later merged with the Bible Standard Church of Eugene, Oregon in 1935 to become the Open Bible Standard Evangelistic Association.[15]

The history of this church is documented in Gotfred S. Bruland, The Origin and Development of the Open Bible Church in Iowa (Des Moines, Iowa: Drake University, M.A. thesis, 1945). A concise account of the origin is found in Kendrick's The Promise Ful-

---

14.   Moore, "Handbook of Denominations," p. 59. George Jeffreys, an English Pentecostal, spells out this doctrinal statute in The Miraculous Four Square Gospel (London: Elim Publishing Co., 1929).

15.   The Bible Standard Church originated from a split with Mrs. Florence Crawford, Apostolic Faith Mission in 1919. The issues of contention at that point were: (1) her church was the only true church; and (2) all divorced persons who had remarried must separate from their present companions before they could become members of the church.

filled, pp. 164-171.

The Oneness Groups

David Reed is currently doing his Ph.D. research at
Boston University on the historical and theological
origins of the "Oneness" or "Jesus Only" movement.
Fred J. Foster's Think It Not Strange, A History of
the Oneness Movement (St. Louis: Pentecostal Publishing House, 1965) and Arthur L. Clanton, United
We Stand (Hazlewood, Mo.: Pentecostal Publishing
House, 1970) are currently the most comprehensive
historical accounts available on this Movement.
Menzies, in Anointed to Serve, chapter six, "The
New Issue" pp. 106-121, gives the most authoritative
description of the movement as it stands in relation
to the Assemblies of God.[16] "The New Issue" was a
controversy regarding the doctrine of the trinity
and the significance of the name Jesus.[17] Synan,

---

16. The Movement hit the Assemblies of God the
     hardest for two reasons. First, as a denomi-
nation they were perhaps the most opposed of all
Pentecostals to strong centrality of power; thus,
they had little control over doctrinal teaching.
Secondly, the teaching hit full force only two
years after they had organized. Many of their
leaders and more than 25% of their ministers embraced the teaching.

17. The distinctive teaching of the "New Issue" is
     best expressed in the Articles of Faith of the
United Pentecostal Church, largest of the Oneness
groups:

"Nature of God"

One true God--revealed Himself as Father,
through His Son in redemption, and as the
Holy Spirit.

The one true God, the Jehovah of the Old
Testament took upon Himself the form of man,
and as son of man was born of the virgin Mary.
God was in Christ reconciling the world unto
himself.

In Him dwelleth all the fullness of the God-

in the Holiness Pentecostal Movement, in a chapter
entitled "Criticism and Controversy" pp. 141-163,
offers the perspective of a disinterested onlooker.
Brumback's Suddenly From Heaven contains a helpful
chapter on the significance of this issue to the
Assemblies of God, pp. 191-215.

When the "New Issue" failed to capture the Assemblies of God, "The Pentecostal Assemblies of the
World" was created in 1916 under the leadership of
G. T. Haywood, a black from Indianapolis. The
group remained bi-racial until 1924, when the white
ministers withdrew to form their own denomination.
Two groups merged in 1945 to form the largest Oneness body "The United Pentecostal Church." A host
of splinter groups exist. For information about
these groups see Clanton's United We Stand. It is
estimated that there are about one-half million
Oneness adherents in the United States.[18] Several
autobiographical and biographical accounts exist of
early leaders in the movement, which are worthy of
note here. These include Frank J. Ewart, The Phenomenon of Pentecost (St. Louis: Pentecostal Publishing House, 1947); Ethel E. Goss, The Winds of

---

head bodily. For it pleased the Father that
in Him should all the fulness dwell.

Therefore Jesus in His humanity was, and is
man, in His deity was, and is God. His flesh
was in the lamb or sacrifice of God, He is
the only mediator between God and man, for
there is one God, and one mediator between
God and man, the man Christ Jesus.

I am the Alpha, Omega, the beginning and
ending, saith the Lord, which is, which was,
and which is to come, the Almighty.

"The Name"

Neither is there salvation in any other, for
there is none other name under heaven given
among men, whereby we must be saved.

Moore, "Handbook of Pentecostal Denominations,"
p. 156.

18. Menzies, Anointed to Serve, p. 120.

God (New York, 1958); Mrs. M. B. Etter, Marvels and Miracles: Signs and Wonders (Indianapolis, 1922); and Sam Officer, Wise Master Builders and the Wheels of Fortune (Cleveland, Tenn.: The Jesus Church, n.d.).

Black Pentecostalism

Today, like the era following the American Revolution and the period following the Russian Revolution in 1917, history books are being rewritten. Black awareness has caused the Negro race to realize that their contribution to American history has been distorted, if not totally ignored.

In seeking to discover their heritage and to establish their identity, many fresh insights are being uncovered. Inevitably in this process some myths are being created as well.

Long ignored by Pentecostals is the role that blacks have played in their origins and development.

The first major study of black contributions is now under way at Vanderbilt, where Garnet Pike is writing a case study entitled,"A Historical Study of Black Pentecostals."

Best materials available to date include Walter J. Hollenweger, "A Black Pentecostal Concept; A Forgotten chapter of Black History," Concept, Special Issue 30, June 1970. (Copies of this may be ordered c/o WCC, 150 Route de Ferney, 1211 Geneva 20, Switzerland.)

Another article is James S. Tinney, "Black Origins of the Pentecostal Movement," Christianity Today, October 8, 1971, pp. 4-6. Finally, Vinson Synan, The Holiness Pentecostal Movement includes an excellent chapter on black contributions: "The Negro Pentecostals," pp. 165-184.

There is little written on individual black denominations. Moore's "Handbook of Pentecostal Denominations" gives a quick sketch of the origins of the major ones.

Mary Mason, The History and Life Work of Bishop C. H. Mason, Chief Apostle, and his Co-laborers (Memphis, n.p., 1934) gives background pertaining to the Church of God in Christ, the largest black Pentecostal denomination.

Another early black Pentecostal group is documented by H. L. Fisher, History of the United Holy Church of America (n.p., n.d.). Like the Church of God in Christ, this group has holiness origins.

The Latter Rain Movement

Among the strongest critics of the Pentecostal Movement at its beginning were the older Holiness denominations and the fundamentalists. The fundamentalists charged that all signs and wonders ceased with the Apostles; therefore, such things as "speaking in other tongues" in the twentieth century were dispensationally impossible. The Pentecostals took this charge seriously, and sought to answer their critics in two ways. First, they appealed to church history, finding various individuals and groups to have experienced "tongues" from time to time throughout the centuries. A second argument was based on what came to be known as the Latter Rain Covenant.[19] This doctrine taught that Joel's prophecy "In the last days I will pour out my Spirit upon all flesh..." had been but partially fulfilled on the Day of Pentecost (Acts 2:16-20), and was to be completed just before Christ's return. Thus, the fact that the Pentecostal revival had occured implied that Christ's second advent was at hand. The fundamentalists were right in saying that supernatural miracles had largely ceased with the first century apostles; but a revival of this should now be expected.

A work that gave great influence to this teaching was David Wesley Myland, The Latter Rain Covenant and Pentecostal Power (Chicago: Evangel Publishing House, 1910). Myland actually used charts of rainfall in Palestine from 1861-1901 to show that rain was increasing in that land. From this data, he concluded that the second coming would occur shortly after 1906.[20]

84

---

19. J. Roswell Flower, "History of the Assemblies of God," pp. 5-6.

20. Synan, Holiness-Pentecostal Movement, p. 146.

This theme was picked up in the late forties by the "New Order of the Latter Rain." Centers of this movement were located at Bethesda Missionary Temple in Detroit, Michigan, pastored by Myrtle Beall, and at Wings of Healing Temple in Portland, Oregon, pastored by Dr. Thomas Wyatt. Israel's establishment as a nation in 1948 was tied to this revival, giving the Latter Rain Movement a great eschatological hope.

Patricia D. Gruits, daughter of Mrs. M. D. Beall, pastor of the Detroit Center gives a theological presentation of this basic belief in Understanding God (Detroit: The Evangel Press, 1962).

Perhaps a sidelight may here be mentioned. This movement has taken seriously Paul's declaration that in Christ there is neither Jew nor Greek, bond nor free, male nor female. Blacks and women both have found responsible roles in the power structure, and unity of spirit is a dynamic reality.

Menzies, Anointed to Serve, pp. 321-325, relates the effect of the movement on the Assemblies of God. Though the two main churches remain strong, the influence of the movement upon Pentecostalism began to wane by the mid-fifties.

Salvationist-Healing Movement

A host of independent, Pentecostal evangelists became prominent during the fifties; although they remained largely outside the Pentecostal denominational structures, they drew their base support from within the Pentecostal denominational ranks. The emphases of their ministries were mass evangelism, divine healing, and deliverance. The impact of these men on the Assemblies of God is documented by Menzies, Anointed to Serve, pp. 330-335.

Best known and most successful of these men is Oral Roberts. In his recent autobiography, The Call (New York: Doubleday & Co., 1972), Roberts describes his ministry as one that set the stage for the rise of the charismatic movement (p. 129). In time his audience gradually drew in more people from main-line denominations. Thus, when the charismatic movement began its sweep in the early sixties, a large number of people had already been oriented to its message. It was a logical conclusion for Roberts, therefore, to leave the Pentecostal Holiness Church and join the United Methodist Church in 1968, and seek to establish himself within the mainstream of historic Christianity.

Several loose evangelistic affiliations have been in existence at one time or another. The best known of these was started by Gordon Lindsay, with headquarters in Dallas, Texas. Through his magazine, The Voice of Healing, the association gained great influence among many Pentecostals. His autobiography, The Gordon Lindsay Story (Dallas: The Voice of Healing Publishing Co., n.d.) and biography, William Branham, a Man Sent From God (Jeffersonville, Ind.: William Branham, 1950) portray the mission he sought to accomplish. Other men who associated with the Voice of Healing at one time or another include Jack Coe, T. L. Osborn, M. A. Daoud, W. V. Grant, and William Caldwell. The organization was revived in 1967 under the name "Christ for the Nations."

Another famous controversial tent evangelist of the era was A. A. Allen. His autobiography, Born to Lose, Bound to Win (Garden City, N. Y.: Doubleday & Co., 1970), provides an interesting account of his ministry.

Carrying on the tradition of Aimee Semple McPherson in the present day has been Kathryn Kuhlman. Her two books, I Believe in Miracles (Englewood Cliffs, N. J.: Prentice-Hall, Inc., 1962) and God Can Do It Again (Englewood Cliffs, N. J.: Prentice-Hall, Inc., 1968) are largely autobiographical. A slightly more controversial book, Alan Spraggett, Kathryn Kuhlman, the Woman Who Believes in Miracles (New York: The World Publishing Co., 1970), assesses her ministry in light of the growing trend of "divine healers" of her day.

Charismatic Movement

Michael Harper, an Englishman, has written the best account tracing the development of the Charismatic Revival in main-line denominations: As at the Beginning: the Twentieth Century Pentecostal Revival (London: Hodder and Stoughton, 1965). A close second is John L. Sherrill, They Speak with Other Tongues (New York: McGraw-Hill Book Co., 1964). In both cases the modern revival is set in the context of classical Pentecostalism. So much has happened in the Movement since these works have been written, however, that they cannot be an adequate guide to the Movement as it now stands.

David J. du Plessis, a former Assemblies of God minister from South Africa, is generally cited for introducing Pentecostalism to the mainline denominations. As a long-time Executive Secretary for the World Pentecostal Conference, du Plessis was in a unique position to contact leaders in the World Council of Churches. He also was the only official Pentecostal observer at the Second Vatican Council, and has since played a large role in the developing Pentecostal Movement among Roman Catholics. His autobiographical The Spirit Bade Me Go: the Astounding Move of God in the Denominational Churches (Oakland, California: David J. du Plessis, 1960) has undergone several revisions and reprintings, and is still available through the author (David J. du Plessis, 3742 Linwood Avenue, Oakland, California, 94602).

Dennis J. Bennett, Nine O'clock in the Morning (Plainfield, N. J.: Logos Press, 1970) is the account of an Anglican who early became involved in the Charismatic Revival. Bennett later teamed with his wife, Rita, to write The Holy Spirit and You (Plainfield, N. J.: Logos Press, 1971), a work that has proved helpful to orient people from other theological traditions to the Pentecostal experience. An important influence in the beginnings of this movement was Trinity Magazine (no longer published), edited by Jean Stone, a member of Bennett's parish in Van Nuys, California.

A host of other books is available; these merely serve to set the others in historical perspective.

The Catholic Pentecostals

J. Gordon Melton, The Catholic Pentecostal Movement (Evanston, Ill.: Garrett Theological Seminary, Nov. 1971) provides the basic bibliography for this section of the Charismatic Movement. Copies are available from the seminary.

Several books on Catholic Pentecostals are well worth mentioning here. The first to appear was Kevin and Dorothy Ranaghan, Catholic Pentecostals (Paramus, N. J.: Paulist Press, 1969). It is an

excellent historical account of the development of
the movement among Catholics. The others: Edward
D. O'Connor, The Pentecostal Movement in the Catholic Church (Notre Dame, Ave Maria Press, 1971);
Donald L. Gelpi, Pentecostalism: A Theological Viewpoint (New York, Paulist Press, 1971); and two books
by J. Massingberd Ford, The Pentecostal Experience,
a New Direction for American Catholics (New York:
Paulist Press, 1970), and Baptism of the Spirit:
Three Essays on the Pentecostal Experience (Techny,
Ill.: Divine Word Publications, 1971), are all attempts to interpret the Pentecostal experience in
light of traditional Roman Catholic theology.

Kilian McDonnell, Executive Director of the Institute for Ecumenical and Cultural Research, College-
ville, Minnesota, presents the best analysis of
what has been happening in a brief essay Catholic
Pentecostalism: Problems in Evaluation (Pecos, New
Mexico: Dove Publications, 1970), a reprint that
originally appeared in Dialog, Winter 1970. McDonnell is seeking to establish his Institute as the
center for future Catholic Pentecostal studies.

The Jesus Movement

Like the rise of classic Pentecostalism, the Jesus
Movement of the late 1960's stands outside the
mainstream of organized Christianity. A host of des-
criptive books is coming off the press. At this
point in history it is impossible to assess the
impact of the Movement, or to predict in what
direction it is heading. Ronald M. Enroth, et al,
The Jesus People (Grand Rapids: Eerdmans, 1972) to
date is the most comprehensive chronicle of the
Movement. William S. Cannon, The Jesus Revolution
(Nashville: Broadman Press, 1971) is an attempt to
assess the Movement in light of evangelical theology.
Jess Moody, The Jesus Freaks (Waco, Texas: Word,
1971) includes a helpful list of communities
throughout the United States. Most of the books
take the form of chronicle accounts of the Movement.
These books include John A. MacDonald, The House of
Acts (Carol Stream, Ill.: Creation House, 1970),
Duane Pederson, Jesus People (Glendale, Calif.:
Regal Books, 1971), Pat King, The Jesus People Are
Coming (Plainfield, N. J.: Logos Press, 1971),
Lowell D. Streiker, The Jesus Trip: Advent of the
Jesus Freaks (Nashville: Abingdon Press, 1971), Ed-
ward Plowman, The Jesus Movement in America (Cool,
1971), Arthur Blessitt, Turned on to Jesus (Haw-

thorn, 1971), and Roger C. Palms, The Jesus Kids
(Valley Forge, Pa.: Judson Press, 1971). Chris-
tianity Today has printed many articles on the
Jesus Movement. These have been compiled in A News
Diary of the Jesus Movement (n.p., 1971).

THEOLOGICAL DISTINCTIVES

A Pentecostal Theology has never actually been
written. Three early attempts, Myer Pearlman,
Knowing the Doctrines of the Bible (Springfield:
Gospel Publishing House, 1937), Ernest S. Williams,
Systematic Theology, 3 Vols. (Springfield, Gospel
Publishing House, 1953), and P. C. Nelson, Bible
Doctrines; A Handbook on Pentecostal Theology (Enid,
Oklahoma: South Western Press, 1936) were based
largely on existing non-Pentecostal works and were
designed to provide a basic structure in theology
for a large number of clergy who had not had the
opportunity of formal training. Carl Brumback
What Meaneth This (Springfield, Mo.: Gospel Publishing House, 1947) perhaps is the best apology
for the Pentecostal distinctives.

89

To date most Pentecostal Bible Colleges are using
theologies written for other traditions in the
training of their ministers.

The Pentecostal Holiness Church is publishing annually the "King Memorial Lecture Series." This is
the most recent expression of Holiness-Pentecostal
theology. The series includes: J. A. Synan, Christian Life in Depth, 1964; H. P. Robinson, Redemption
Conceived and Revealed, 1965; B. E. Underwood, The
Gifts of the Spirit, 1967; Noel Brooks; Scriptural
Holiness, 1967; J. A. Synan, The Shape of Things to
Come, 1969; and B. E. Underwood, The Spirit's Sword,
1969. All are published by Advocate Press in
Franklin Springs, Georgia.

The Holy Spirit

The largest emphasis, of course, is on the work of
the Holy Spirit. Here the most recent books in the
field are written by non-Pentecostals. Frederick
Dale Bruner, A Theology of the Holy Spirit, the
Pentecostal Experience and the New Testament Witness
(Grand Rapids: Eerdmans, 1970), and James D. G. Dunn,
Baptism in the Holy Spirit: a Reexamination of the
New Testament Teaching of the Gift of the Spirit in

Relation to Pentecostalism Today (Naperville, Ill.:
Allenson, 1970). Dunn's work is largely a Biblical
study while Bruner divides his work in two sections,
dealing first with the Pentecostal understanding of
the doctrine as it developed historically, then
moving in to consider the Biblical evidence. Bruner
includes a helpful appendix of documents upon which
the Pentecostal doctrine of the Holy Spirit is based.
He also provides a short informative bibliographical
essay on the existing works that are relevant to his
book, and finally, his extensive bibliography is
worthy of note.

No one Pentecostal theologian has gained wider acceptance among the Pentecostal denominations than
the Englishman, Donald Gee. The Ministry Gifts of
Christ (Springfield: Gospel Publishing House, 1930),
Concerning Spiritual Gifts (Springfield: Gospel Publishing House, 1937), and Spiritual Gifts in the
Work of the Ministry Today (Springfield: Gospel Pub-
lishing House, 1963) are probably his best known
writings on the work of the Holy Spirit. The influ-
ence of other writers has been limited primarily to
their own denominations. These include Harold
Horton, The Gifts of the Spirit (Luten, England:
Redemption Tidings Bookroom, 1934) and The Baptism
of the Holy Spirit (London: Victory Press, 1956),
Ralph M. Riggs, The Spirit Himself (Springfield:
Gospel Publishing House, 1949), Myer Pearlman, The
Heavenly Gift: Studies in the Work of the Holy
Spirit (Springfield: Gospel Publishing House, 1935),
Aimee Semple McPherson, The Baptism of the Holy
Spirit (Los Angeles: Four Square Gospel, 1928),
George Jeffreys, Pentecostal Rays: The Baptism and
the Gifts of the Spirit (Minneapolis: Northern Gos-
pel Publishing House, 1946), Melvin L. Hodges,
Spiritual Gifts (Springfield: Gospel Publishing
House, 1964), W. H. Turner, The Difference Between
Regeneration, Sanctification and the Pentecostal
Baptism (Franklin Springs, Ga.: Publishing House of
the Pentecostal Holiness Church, 1947), J. H. King,
From Passover to Pentecost (Franklin Springs, Ga.:
Publishing House of the Pentecostal Holiness Church,
1914), and Bennie S. Triplett, A Contemporary Study
of the Holy Spirit (Cleveland, Tenn.: Pathway Press,
1970).

Frank J. Ewart, The Revelation of Jesus Christ (St.
Louis: Pentecostal Publishing House, n.d.) provides
the best theological defense for the "Oneness" doctrine. The teaching is refuted in Carl Brumback,
God in Three Persons (Cleveland, Tenn.: Pathway

Press, 1959).

The early Pentecostals drew heavily on prominent
Holiness leaders of the late nineteenth century and
early twentieth century in formulating their the-
ology of the Holy Spirit. Representative titles
of this era include R. A. Torrey, The Holy Spirit
(Westwood, N. J.: Fleming H. Revell Co., 1927),
Andrew Murray, The Full Blessing of Pentecost
(Westwood, N. J.: Fleming H. Revell Co., 1908), A.
J. Gordon, The Ministry of the Spirit (New York:
Fleming H. Revell, 1894), A. B. Simpson, The Holy
Spirit, 2 Vols. (Harrisburg, Pa.: Christian Publi-
cations Inc., n.d.), and Charles G. Finney, Power
from on High (London: Victory Press, 1944).

Glossolalia

From the outset, the Pentecostal teaching which met
the most controvery has been the association of
glossolalia with the baptism in the Holy Spirit.
The most exhaustive study of this phenomenon is
Lincoln M. Vivier's unpublished M.D. thesis,
"Glossolalia" (Johannesburg: University of Wit-
watersrand, 1960). Vivier studies the Biblical
evidence and the historical occurrence of tongues
before the twentieth century. He then considers a
host of case studies, and concludes that Pentecostals tend to be slightly above average in their
psychological adjustment. The best overview from a
Pentecostal perspective is Wade Horton, ed., The
Glossolalia Phenomenon (Cleveland, Tenn.: Pathway
Press, 1966), a compilation of articles by prominent Pentecostals. It treats the phenomenon in its
historical and theological aspects. The classic
Biblical exegesis from a Pentecostal point of view
is William G. MacDonald, Glossolalia in the New
Testament (Springfield, Mo.: Gospel Publishing House,
1964) a reprint of an article first appearing in
the Evangelical Theological Society Bulletin
7:59-68, Spring, 1964.[21] A significant early work

---

21. An excellent supplement to this is Anthony
    Palma "Tongues and Prophecy: a Comparative
Study in Charismata" (St. Louis: Concordia Theological Seminary, 1966), an unpublished S.T.M. dissertation. Palma's analysis brings him to the conclusion that the purpose of glossolalia is praise.

is Robert C. Dalton, Tongues Like as of Fire: a Critical Study of Modern Tongues Movements in the Light of Apostolic and Patristic Times (Springfield, Mo.: Gospel Publishing House, 1945).

As glossolalia became prominent in mainline denominations, church leaders were at a loss as to how to handle the situation. The first official response in the Protestant Episcopal Church was a Pastoral Letter Regarding Speaking in Tongues by the late Bishop James A. Pike of California. The text of this letter appeared in Pastoral Psychology 15: 56-61, May 1964. A second official pronouncement is a Report on Glossolalia (Minneapolis, Minn.: Commission of Evangelism of the American Lutheran Church, 1964). A third is the Report of the Special Committee on the Work of the Holy Spirit (Philadelphia: United Presbyterian Church of the U.S.A., 1970).

All are efforts to give guidance to all parties concerned when glossolalia appears in the local church.

A host of psychological and theological studies have been written on glossolalia. Most recent is John P. Kildahl, The Psychology of Speaking in Tongues (New York: Harper & Row, 1972). Dr. Kildahl, on the faculty at the New York Post Graduate Center for Mental Health, and a member of the investigating commission for the American Lutheran Church, has spent over ten years studying glossolalia. He offers a sympathetic ear to those who participate in the phenomenon, but concludes that, if speaking in tongues is to be understood as a gift of the Spirit, it must be in terms of how it is used, not by the mere fact that it occurs.

Helpful in Kildahl's work is an anlysis of several of the leading monographs that have been written in the field. Morton T. Kelsey, Tongues Speaking: An Experiment in Spiritual Experience (Garden City, N. Y.: Doubleday & Co., 1964), George Barton Cutten, Speaking with Tongues, Historically and Psychologically Considered (New Haven, Conn.: Yale University Press, 1927), Ira J. Martin, Glossolalia in the Apostolic Church; A Survey Study of Tongues Speech (Berea, Ky.: Berea College, 1960), Wayne E. Oates and others, Glossolalia Tongue Speaking in Biblical, Historical and Psychological Perspective (Nashville: Abingdon Press, 1967), all treat the glossolalia phenomenon primarily from a psychological point of view. Also to be noted at this point is a significant article, James N. Lapsley and John H. Simpson,

"Speaking in Tongues: Token of Group Acceptance and Divine Approval," Pastoral Psychology, XV (May 1964), 48-53, and "Speaking in Tongues: Infantile Babble," Pastoral Psychology, XV (September 1964), 16-24. Each of these works is written by outside observers, whose attitudes toward the experience range from sympathy to hostility. William J. Samarin, Tongues of Men and Angels (New York: Macmillan, 1972) is perhaps the best linguistic study of the glossolalia phenomenon.

An account of an investigator who became personally involved in the experience is John L. Sherrill, They Speak with Other Tongues (New York: McGraw-Hill, 1964). A similar account of an earlier investigation is Elmer C. Miller, Pentecost Examined by a Baptist Lawyer (Springfield, Mo.: Gospel Publishing House, 1936).

Works critical of the present phenomenon from a theological viewpoint include Robert G. Gromacki, The Modern Tongues Movement (Philadelphia: Presbyterian and Reformed Publishing Co., 1967), Anthony A. Hoekema, What About Tongue-Speaking? (Grand Rapids: Eerdmans Publishing Co., 1966), Donald W. Burdick, Tongues: To Speak or Not To Speak (Chicago: Moody Press, 1969), Donald S. Metz, Speaking in Tongues: An Analysis (Kansas City, Mo.: Nazarene Publishing House, 1964), and H. J. Stolee, Speaking in Tongues (Minneapolis: Augsburg Publishing House, 1963). A positive presentation is by a Lutheran , Laurence Christenson, Speaking in Tongues and its Significance for the Church (Minneapolis: Bethany Fellowship, 1968). W. H. Turner, Pentecost and Tongues (Franklin Springs, Ga.: Advocate Press, 1968) supplies the latest thinking among classic Pentecostals on the issue.

Divine Healing

A third emphasis in the Pentecostal Movement has been divine healing. This emphasis received its impetus from the leader of the Christian and Missionary Alliance, A. B. Simpson. Simpson's views on healing are best expressed in his book, The Gospel of Healing (New York: Christian Alliance Publishing Co., 1915). Also influential was Smith Wigglesworth, Ever Increasing Faith (Springfield, Mo.: Gospel Publishing House, 1924) and A. J. Gordon, The Ministry of Healing or, Miracles of Cure in All Ages (New York: Revell, 1882). This was reprinted in 1961 by Christian Publications, Harrisburg, Pennsylvania. F. F. Bosworth, Christ the Healer (Racine, Wis.: n.p., 1927) defended the position: faith is always rewarded with healing. This position influenced thousands of Pentecostals for years.

Donald Gee, Concerning Spiritual Gifts (Springfield, Mo.: Gospel Publishing House, n.d.) and George Jeffreys, Healing Rays (London: Henry E. Walter, Ltd., 1952) are standard works.[22]

The more prolific writers on divine healing have quite naturally been the faith evangelists who gained popularity during the fifties and early sixties. The best of these are T. L. Osborn, Healing the Sick and Casting Out Devils (Tulsa: T. L. Osborn Evangelistic Association, 1955) and Oral Roberts, If You Need Healing, Do These Things (Tulsa: Oral Roberts, 1947). Roberts' work went through several editions and has been revised considerably each time. Other examples of this literature include Gordon Lindsay, World Evangelism Now by Healing and Miracles (Glendale, California: Church Press, 1951); William Caldwell, Meet the Healer (Tulsa: Miracle Moments Evangelistic Association, Inc., 1965); A. A. Allen, God's Guarantee to Heal You (Dallas: A. A. Allen, 1950); W. V. Grant, Divine Healing Answers, 2 Vols. (Waxahachie, Texas: Southwestern Bible Institute Press, 1952); Tommy Hicks, Manifest Deliverance for You Now (Lancaster, California: Tommy Hicks, 1952); Theodore Fitch, Our Afflictions: Cause and Remedy (Council Bluffs, Iowa: Theodore Fitch, n.d.); and Thomas Wyatt, A Study in Healing and Deliverance, 2 Vols. (Los Angeles: Wings of Healing, n.d.).

For a more complete listing of the writings of these men consult the "Bibliography on Divine Healing," compiled by Juanita Raudzus, available at Oral Ro-

---

22. Gee's work in particular has had great influence among Pentecostal circles. This has been due to the Pentecostal teaching that divine healing is in the atonement: "By whose stripes we are healed" (I Peter 2:24). Gee's ministry has served as a corrective to the popular, though unofficial, idea that one without faith to experience divine healing cannot be sure of his salvation either.

berts University for $1.00.

Though the faith evangelists have taken the lead in
this area, the Pentecostal denominations have also
produced a number of titles worthy of note. These
works include James A. Cross, Healing in the Church
(Cleveland, Tenn.: Pathway Press, 1962); Hart R.
Armstrong, Divine Healing, 2 Vols. (Springfield,
Mo.: Gospel Publishing House, 1948); William H.
Turner, Christ the Great Physician (Franklin Springs,
Ga.: Advocate Press, 1941); Noel Brooks, Sickness,
Health and God (Franklin Springs, Ga.: Advocate
Press, n.d.); and Gordon F. Atter, The Student's
Handbook on Divine Healing (Peterborough, Ontario:
The Book Nook, 1960).

Women have played a prominent role in the Healing
ministry of the Pentecostal Movement. Aimee Semple
McPherson's teaching is illustrated in her Divine
Healing Sermons (Los Angeles: International Church
of the Four Square Gospel, n.d.). Kathryn Kuhlman,
I Believe in Miracles (Englewood Cliffs, N. J.:
Prentice Hall, Inc., 1962) and God Can Do It Again
(Englewood Cliffs, N. J.: Prentice Hall, Inc., 1969
are contemporary expressions of the impact of the
Divine Healing teaching. The chief proponent of
the "Healing of the Memories" concept, Agnes Sanford, has published several works of note. Best
known is The Healing Light (St. Paul, Minn.: Macalester Park Publishing Co., 1947). Other of her
writings include Behold Your God (St. Paul, Minn.:
Macalester Park Publishing Co., 1958), The Healing
Gifts of the Spirit (Philadelphia: J. B. Lippincott
Co., 1966), and The Healing Power of the Bible
(Philadelphia: J. B. Lippincott Co., 1969). Also
worthy of mention is Anne S. White, Healing Adven-
ture (London: Arthur Janes, Ltd., 1969) and Day-
spring (Plainfield, N. J.: Logos Press, 1972). Mrs.
White is one of Sanford's best known disciples, and
is considered by many to be her successor.

A helpful analysis of the whole healing phenomenon
is George Bishop, Faith Healing: God or Fraud?
(Los Angeles: Sherbourne Press, Inc., 1967). A
final work on healing should be noted, Gilbert W.
Kirby, The Question of Healing; Some Thoughts on
Healing and Suffering (London: Victory Press, 1967).
This work is a collection of articles by men repre-
sentative of most branches of the Christian Faith.
One is enabled to view the Pentecostal position on
Divine Healing in light of the teaching of the
whole church.

Special Issues

The "Deliverance Ministry" (exorcism or the casting
out of demons) has long played a role in Pentecostal
circles. Oral Roberts, Deliverance from Fear and
From Sickness (Tulsa: Oral Roberts, 1954) represents the early teaching on the subject. The doctrine was developed through the faith evangelists
associated with The Voice of Healing. The teaching
and practice are now being expressed in the Charismatic Movement, largely through the influence of
the Holy Spirit Teaching Mission of Fort Lauderdale,
Florida. Leaders Derek Prince, Bob Mumford, Charles
Simpson and Don Basham's writings appear in the
periodical New Wine, and less frequently in the
Logos Journal.

Prophecy has been another interest of Pentecostals
from their beginnings. Frank M. Boyd, long-time
Assemblies of God Bible school teacher, has been the
guiding influence of this interest. Ages and Dis-
pensations (Springfield, Mo.: Gospel Publishing
House, 1949) and Introduction to Prophecy (Springfield, Mo.: Gospel Publishing House, 1948) are his
best known works. In addition to these, he has
published several commentaries on the Old Testament
prophets.

Donald N. Bowdle has just written a perceptive
study of regeneration as preparatory to the baptism
with the Holy Spirit: Redemption Accomplished and
Applied: a Study in the Doctrine of Salvation
(Cleveland, Tenn.: Pathway Press, 1972).

William G. MacDonald has offered a Pentecostal concept of the doctrine of the Church, "A People in
Community: Theological Interpretation," which appears in a book edited by James L. Garrett, The Concept of the Believers' Church (Scottdale, Pa.: Herald Press, 1969, pp. 143-164) based on the papers
delivered in Louisville, Kentucky at the 1967 conference on the concept of the Believers' Church.
MacDonald stands with Dietrich Bonhoeffer, The Communion of Saints; a Dogmatic Inquiry into the So-
ciology of the Church (New York: Harper and Row,
1963) and against Ernest Troeltsch, in arguing that
the Church is a community of faith, rather than a
society.

A sociological study of Pentecostalism which must
be noted is William W. Wood, Culture and Personality;
Aspects of the Pentecostal Holiness Religion (The

Hague: Mouton Co., 1965).

MISSIONS

Another major emphasis of Pentecostals has been
missions. Walter J. Hollenweger, The Pentecostals,
as one would expect, gives the most comprehensive
coverage of the impact Pentecostals have made
throughout the world. Charles W. Conn, Where the
Saints Have Trod; a History of Church of God Missions (Cleveland, Tenn.: Pathway Press, 1959),
Serena M. Hodges, Look on the Fields; a Missionary
Survey (Springfield, Mo.: Gospel Publishing House,
1963), and Noel Perkin and John Garlock, Our World
Witness (Springfield, Mo.: Gospel Publishing House,
1965) represent the best denominational sources
available.

Lester F. Sumrall, Through Blood and Fire in Latin
America (Grand Rapids: Zondervan, 1944) and Christian Lalive D'Epiney, Haven of the Masses; a Study
of the Pentecostal Movement in Chile (London: Lut-
terworth Press, 1969) are exemplary of literature
written on particular areas. Steve Durasoff, The
Russian Protestants (Cranbury, N. J.: Associated
University Press, 1969) contains three chapters on
the Russian Pentecostals which provide a rare insight of what is going on behind the Iron Curtain.

Melvin L. Hodges, The Indigenous Church (Springfield, Mo.: Gospel Publishing House, 1953) spells
out the Pentecostal philosophy of missions. Hodges
argues much like Donald A. McGavran, Understanding
Church Growth (Grand Rapids: Eerdmans, 1970), break-
ing away from the compound concept of Christian
world missions.

Two representative biographies of Pentecostal missions are Lester Sumrall, Lillian Trasher; Nile
Mother (Springfield, Mo.: Gospel Publishing House,
1951), and Angeline Tucker, He is in Heaven (New
York: McGraw Hill Book Co., 1965). Miss Trasher
broke her engagement with her fiancee to run an or-
phanage in Egypt, while Jay Tucker became a martyr
during the Congo civil war in the mid-sixties.

HOMILETICS AND SERMONS

Two books on preaching best representing Pentecostal efforts are Guy P. Duffield, Pentecostal Preach-

ing (New York: Vantage Press, 1957) and C. L. Allen,
Pentecostal Preaching is Different (Los Angeles: B.
N. Robertson, 1961). Both developed out of an an-
nual lectureship series on preaching held at L.I.F.E.
Bible College.[23] H. P. Robinson Heaven's Quest
for a Man Like God (Franklin Springs, Ga.: Advocate
Press, 1969) also offers insights in preaching from
a Pentecostal perspective.

The best known sermon collection in Pentecostal
ranks is C. M. Ward, Revivaltime Sermons (Springfield, Mo.: Gospel Publishing House, 1953-) based
on his weekly radio broadcasts. The Pentecostal
Pulpit (Springfield, Mo.: Gospel Publishing House),
an earlier series published by the Assemblies of God,
should also be mentioned here.

Most of the titles mentioned in the theology section
are published sermons. In addition to these, im-
portant representative early works include N. J.
Holmes, Life Sketches and Sermons (Royston, Ga.:
Press of the Pentecostal Holiness Church, 1920),
Robert L. Parham, comp., Selected Sermons of the
Late Charles F. Parham and Sarah E. Parham (Joplin,
Mo.: Robert L. Parham, 1941), F. M. Britton, Pentecostal Truth; or Sermons on Regeneration, Sanctification, the Baptism of the Holy Spirit, Divine Healing, the Second Coming of Jesus, etc. (Royston, Ga.:
Publishing House of the Pentecostal Holiness Church,
1919), J. H. King, Christ, God's Love Gift (Franklin
Springs, Ga.: Advocate Press, 1969), and G. F. Taylor, The Second Coming (Franklin Springs, Ga.: Advocate Press, 1950).

APOLOGETICS

Several books have been written to set forth Pen-
tecostal belief and practice to the non-Pentecostal
world. The Church of God (Cleveland, Tennessee)
has produced by far the greatest number: Ray H.
Hughes, Church of God Distinctives (Cleveland, Tenn.:
Pathway Press, 1968), What is Pentecost? (Cleveland,
Tenn.: Pathway Press, 1963), Earl P. Paulk, Your
Pentecostal Neighbor (Cleveland, Tenn.: Pathway
Press, 1958), and Frank W. Lemons, Our Pentecostal

---

23. L.I.F.E. is the Bible College of the Inter-
    national Church of the Four Square Gospel.

Heritage (Cleveland, Tenn.: Pathway Press, 1961).

Other works include M. A. Tomlinson, Basic Bible Beliefs (Cleveland, Tenn.: White Wing Publishing House, 1961), and United Pentecostal Church, What We Believe and Teach (St. Louis: Pentecostal Publishing House, n.d.).

Though always careful to maintain their distinctives, Pentecostals have felt a growing affinity with Evangelical Christianity. One tangible result of this has been Russell P. Spittler's book Cults and Isms; Twenty Alternatives to Evangelical Christianity (Grand Rapids: Baker Book House, 1962).

APPENDIX A

A List of Pentecostal Denominations

The following list of Pentecostal churches appeared in Everett L. Moore, Handbook of Pentecostal Denominations in the
United States. Statistics given are taken from the 1972
edition of Yearbook of American Churches and the 5th edition [1970] of Frank Mead, Handbook of Protestant Denominations in the United States where available. Moore's figures
are kept in a few cases. Obviously, some of these figures
are inaccurate. However, the listing does provide the com-
parative size of the denominations when grouped by doctrinal
distinctives.

Holiness Pentecostal Denominations:	Churches	Membership
Apostolic Faith Mission	44	4,835
Church of God (Cleveland, Tenn.)	4,024	272,276
Church of God in Christ	4,500	425,000
Church of God of Prophecy	1,561	51,527
Church of God (Mountain Assembly)	100	3,500
Church of God (World Headquarters)	2,025	75,890
Congregational Holiness Church	147	4,859
Emmanuel Holiness Church	56	1,200
Fire Baptized Holiness Church of God in America	300	6,000
International Pentecostal Assemblies	60	6,500
Original Church of God	70	20,000
Pentecostal Church of Christ	43	1,209
Pentecostal Fire Baptized Holiness Church	41	545
Pentecostal Free Will Baptists	150	13,500
Pentecostal Holiness Church	1,324	69,679
United Holy Church of America	470	28,980
TOTALS: 16 Denominations	14,915	985,500

Keswick Pentecostal Denominations:	Churches	Membership
Assemblies of God	8,734	670,000
California Evangelistic Association	50	4,000
Calvary Pentecostal Church	22	8,000
Christian Church of North America	110	10,000
Elim Missionary Assemblies	60	3,500
House of David	66	40,816
Independent Assemblies of God	136	--
International Church of the Four Square Gospel	741	89,215
Open Bible Standard Churches	275	30,000
Pentecostal Church of God of America	975	115,000
United Full Gospel Churches	50	--
United Fundamentalist Church	300	--
World Church	--	--
Zion Evangelistic Fellowship	96	10,000
TOTALS: 14 Denominations	11,615	980,531

Jesus Only (Oneness) Pentecostal Denominations:	Churches	Membership
Apostolic Church	--	--
Apostolic Overcoming Holy Church of God	300	75,000
Associated Brotherhood of Christians	40	2,500
Church of our Lord Jesus Christ of the Apostolic Faith	155	45,000
Full Salvation Union	--	--
Jesus Church	--	--
Pentecostal Assemblies of the World	550	45,000
United Pentecostal Church	2,400	250,000
TOTALS: 8 Denominations	3,445	417,500

APPENDIX B

Major Pentecostal Publishing Houses in the United States

1. Advocate Press, P.O. Box 98, Franklin Springs, Ga. 30639 (Pentecostal Holiness)
2. Congregational Holiness Publishing House, Griffin, Ga. 30223
3. Echo Park Evangelistic Association, 1100 Glendale Blvd., Los Angeles, California 90026 (International Church of the Four Square Gospel)
4. Gospel Publishing House, 1445 Boonville Ave., Springfield, Mo. 65802 (Assemblies of God)
5. Logos International, 185 N. Ave., Plainfield, N.J. 07060 (Independent)
6. Pathway Press, 1080 Montgomery Ave., Cleveland, Tenn. 37311 (Church of God, Cleveland, Tenn.)
7. Pentecostal Publishing House, 3645 S. Grand Blvd., St. Louis, Mo. 63418 (United Pentecostal Church)
8. Voice of Healing Publishing Co., P.O. Box 8658, Dallas, Texas 75216 (Christ for the Nations)
9. White Wing Publishing House, Keith St., Cleveland, Tenn. 37311 (Church of God of Prophecy)

APPENDIX C

Pentecostal Periodicals

Vinson Synan suggests that the Pentecostal Movement was
spread worldwide largely due to the wide spread coverage
it received in the Holiness Periodicals.[24]

The following lists suggest the Pentecostals have learned
the importance of periodical literature as an avenue for
perpetuating their heritage.

A more extensive listing of Pentecostal Periodicals,
Juanita Walker, A Bibliography of the Pentecostal Periodical Holdings in the Oral Roberts University Collection,
(Tulsa, Oklahoma: Oral Roberts University) can be ob-
tained from the university for $3.00. Walker's bibliogra-
phy takes the format of Ulrich's International Periodical
Directory listing addresses, frequency of publication and
subscription rates where relevant. No effort has been
made to include inclusive dates of ORU's holdings.

I Early Pentecostal Periodicals[25]

*1. The Apostolic Faith. Bi-monthly, edited by Charles
    F. Parham; later by E. N. Bell.
*2. Apostolic Faith. Los Angeles. William J. Seymour,
    editor.
*3. Apostolic Faith. Portland, Oregon. Florence Craw-
    ford, editor.
*4. Apostolic Messenger. Toronto, Canada. A. H. Argue.
*5. The Christian Evangel. J. Roswell Flower, editor.
    Plainfield, Ind. Weekly.
*6. Latter Rain Evangel. William H. Piper, pastor of the
    Stone Church in Chicago. Monthly.
*7. Pentecostal Testimony. William Durham, editor.
*8. Sampson's Foxes. A. J. Tomlinson. Monthly.
*9. Tried by Fire. Topeka, Kansas. Herbert & Lillie
    Buffum. Monthly.
*10. Word and Witness. Melvern, Arkansas. Edited by
    M. M. Pinson; later E. N. Bell. 1913-1916.

II Official Organs of Classic Pentecostal Denominations

1. Advocate, Advocate Press, Pentecostal Holiness, P.O.
   Box 98, Franklin Springs, Ga. 30639, bi-weekly. $2.00.
2. Bridegroom's Messenger, International Pentecostal Assemblies, 892 Berne St., S. E., Atlanta, Ga., 30316, monthly.

---

24. Vinson Synan, The Relationship of the Holiness Move-
     ment to the Pentecostal Movement (Wilmore, Ky.: As-
bury Theological Seminary, May 2, 1972, p. 4, unpublished
lecture).
25. *Periodical has ceased publication.

3. Calvary Tidings, Calvary Pentecostal Church, Olympia, Washington. Monthly.
4. The Church of God, Church of God World Headquarters, 9305 224th St., Queens Village, New York, 11428, bi-monthly. $1.50.
5. Church of God Evangel, Pathway Press, 1080 Montgomery Ave., Cleveland, Tenn., 37311, bi-monthly. $3.00.
6. Elim Pentecostal Herald, Elim Missionary Assemblies, Lima, New York. Monthly.
7. Four Square World Advance, International Church of the Four Square Gospel, 1100 Glendale Blvd., Los Angeles, Cal., 90026, monthly. Formerly Foursquare Magazine until 1964.
8. Gospel Herald, Church of God of the Mountain Assembly, Jellico, Tenn., monthly. $1.50.
9. Gospel Messenger, Congregational Holiness Church, Box 290, Griffin, Ga., 30223, monthly. $1.50.
10. Harvest Time, United Pentecostal Church, Inc., 3645 S. Grand Blvd., St. Louis, Mo., 63118.
11. Herald of Faith, Independent Assemblies of God, San Diego, Cal., monthly.
12. The Herald, Church of God of Apostolic Faith, 2200 W. Edison, Tulsa, Oklahoma, 74103. Ceased publication May 1966.
13. Light of Hope, The Apostolic Faith, N. W. and Burnside, Portland, Ore., 97209, bi-monthly. Formerly The Apostolic Faith to 1966.
14. Light of the World, The Jesus Church, Box 652, Cleveland, Tenn., 37311, quarterly. $2.00.
15. Message of the Open Bible, Open Bible Standard Churches, 1159 24th St., Des Moines, Iowa, 50311, bi-monthly. $2.00.
16. The Messenger, (Original) Church of God, Chattanooga, Tenn. Semi-monthly.
17. The Pentecostal Evangel, Gospel Publishing House, Assemblies of God, 1445 Boonville Ave., Springfield, Mo., 65802, weekly. $4.00.
18. Pentecostal Free-Will Baptist Messenger, Pentecostal Free-Will Baptist Messenger, Box 966, Dunn, N. C. Monthly. $2.00.
19. Pentecostal Herald, United Pentecostal Church, 3645 S. Grand Blvd., St. Louis, Mo., 63418, monthly. $2.00.
20. Pentecostal Messenger, Pentecostal Church of America, Box 850, Joplin, Mo., 64801, monthly. $2.00.
21. White Wing Messenger, White Wing Publishing House, Cleveland, Tenn., 37311, weekly. $2.50.
22. Wings of Truth, Church of God of Prophecy, Box 5535, Roanoke, Va., 24012, monthly. $1.50.

III <u>Periodicals of Salvationist-Faith Healing Evangelists</u>

1. <u>Abundant Life</u>, Oral Roberts Evangelisitic Association,
   P.O. Box 2187, Tulsa, Oklahoma, 74105. Formerly
   <u>Healing Waters</u>, changed Sept., 1953; <u>America's Healing</u>
   <u>Magazine</u>, changed Jan., 1956; <u>Healing</u>, changed 1956.
   Monthly. $1.00.
2. <u>Christ for the Nations</u>, Voice of Healing Pub. Co., P.O.
   Box 8658, Dallas, Texas, 75216, monthly. Formerly
   <u>Voice of Healing</u> through April, 1967.
3. <u>The Christian Challenge</u>, Coe Foundations, Inc., Box
   8538, Dallas, Texas, 75216, monthly. Formerly
   <u>Herald of Healing</u> and <u>International Healing</u> to June,
   1962.
4. <u>Deeper Life</u>, Morris Cerulla World Evangelism, Inc.,
   4455 Lamont, Box 9525, San Diego, Cal., 92109, monthly.
   $2.00.
5. <u>Faith Digest</u>, T. L. Osborn Evangelistic Assn., 1400
   E. Skelly Dr., Tulsa, Oklahoma, 74102, monthly.
6. <u>Full Gospel News</u>, Full Gospel Evangelisitic Assn., Box
   431, Webb City, Mo., 64870, monthly.
7. <u>The Healing Messenger</u>, Bible Revival Evangelistic
   Assn., David Nunn, evangelist. 6626 S. R. L. Thornton
   Fwy., Dallas, Texas, 75208, monthly.
8. <u>Latter Rain Evangel</u>, Bethesda Missionary Temple, 7570
   E. Nevada Ave., Detroit, Mich., 48234.
9. <u>The March of Faith</u>, Wings of Healing, Inc., Thomas
   Wyatt, 847 S. Grand Ave., Los Angeles, Cal., 90017,
   monthly. $1.00.
10. Miracle Magazine, A. A. Allen Revivals, Inc., Miracle
    Valley, Ariz., monthly.
11. <u>Miracles and Missions Digest</u>, Voice of Miracle and
    Missions, Inc., M. A. Daud, Box 5646, Dallas, Texas,
    75222, monthly.
12. <u>Revival of America</u>, Leroy Jenkins Evangelisitic Assn.,
    Inc., Box F, Delaware, Ohio, 43015, monthly. $1.00.
13. <u>Voice of Deliverance</u>, International Deliverance
    Churches, Jester and Davis St., Dallas, Texas, 75211,
    monthly.
14. <u>A Voice of Faith</u>, Faith Temple Church, Inc., Amman
    Grubb, Box 3220, Memphis, Tenn., 38101, monthly.
15. <u>Word of Faith</u>, Hagin Evangelisitic Assn., Box 50126,
    Tulsa, Oklahoma, 74150, monthly.

IV <u>Charismatic Periodicals</u>

*1. <u>Charisma Digest</u>, Full Gospel Business Men's Fellowship,
    Int., 836 S. Figueroa St., Los Angeles, Cal., 90017.
    Semi-annual. $1.00. Discontinued, Jan. 22, 1970.
2. <u>Cross and the Switchblade</u>, Teen Challenge Publications,
   Box 161, New York, N. Y., 11238. Bi-monthly.
3. <u>Heartbeat</u>, Charismatic Educational Centers, Inc., 1730
   S. W. 22nd Ave., Fort Lauderdale, Fla., 33312. Monthly.

APPENDIX C (continued)

4. Logos Journal, Logos International, 185 N. Ave., Plainfield, N. J., 07060. Bi-monthly. $3.00.
5. New Covenant, Charismatic Revival Service P.O. Box 102,
   Main Street Station, Ann Arbor, Mich., 48107. Monthly.
   $5.00.
6. New Nation News, Children of God, Texas Soul Clinic,
   Rt. 1, Mingus, Texas, 76463.
7. New Wine, Holy Spirit Teaching Missions, 1730 S. W.
   22nd Ave., Fort Lauderdale, Fla., 33312. Monthly.
8. Trinity, Blessed Trinity Society, Box 2422, Van Nuys,
   Cal. Quarterly. $5.00. Publication ceased Feb., 1966.
9. Voice, Full Gospel Business Men's Fellowship International, 836 S. Figueron St., Los Angeles, Cal., 90017.
   Monthly. $1.00.

V Missions

1. Full Gospel Native Missionary, Full Gospel Native
   Missionary Assn., Box 1240 Joplin, Mo., 64801. Monthly.
2. Global Witness, United Pentecostal Church, 8855 Dunn
   Road, Hazelwood, Mo., 63042. Monthly.
3. Good News Crusades Assemblies of God, 1445 Boonville
   Ave., Springfield, Mo., 65802. Bi-monthly. Formerly
   Global Conquest through August, 1967.
4. The Missionary Voice, Pentecostal Church of God of
   America, Inc., 316 Joplin St., Box 816, Joplin, Mo.
   Monthly.
5. Voice of Revival, Missionary Evangelism, Inc., 1601
   Linda Drive, Decatur, Ga., 30032. Monthly.
6. World Evangelism, American Evangelistic Assn., Box
   4326, Dallas, Texas, 75224. Monthly.
7. World Harvest, World Temples, Inc., Lester Sumrall,
   Box 12, South Bend, Ind., 46624. Monthly.
8. World Vision, Open Bible Standard Churches, 851 19th
   St., Des Moines, Iowa. Quarterly.
9. World o Rama, Pentecostal Holiness Church, Franklin
   Springs, Ga., 30639. Quarterly.

VI Scholarly Journals and Interdenominational Newsletters

1. Academic Forum, Pathway Press, Church of God. 1080
   Montgomery Ave., Cleveland, Tenn., 37311. Quarterly.
2. Paraclete, Gospel Publishing House, Assemblies of God,
   1445 Boonville Ave., Springfield, Mo., 65802. Quarterly. $2.50.

APPENDIX C   (continued)

VII   <u>International and Interdenominational Publications</u>

*1. <u>Pentecost</u>, World Conference of Pentecostal Churches,
    36-37 Clapham Crescent, London, S. W. 4, England.
    Quarterly.   Ceased publication 1966.
 2. <u>P. F. N. A. News</u>, Pentecostal Fellowship of North
    America, 1445 Boonville Ave., Springfield, Mo.,
    65802.   Quarterly.
 3. <u>Society for Pentecostal Studies Newsletter</u>, Emmanuel
    College, Box 122, Franklin Springs, Ga., 30639.
    Quarterly. $3.00.
 4. <u>World Pentecost</u>, World Conference of Pentecostal
    Churches.   The City Temple, Cowbridge Road, Cardiff,
    Wales, Great Britain.   Quarterly. $3.00.

APPENDIX   D

Co-operative Pentecostal Bodies

1. World Pentecostal Fellowship

The WPF was organized in Zurich, Switzerland, in 1947 under
the influence of European Pentecostal Leaders. All Pentecostal groups in the world are eligible to send representa-
tives. The purpose of the meetings is for spiritual fellowship and growth. No form of binding legislation is
attempted. The official journal, Pentecost, ceased publication in 1966 at the death of the editor, Donald Gee.
A new publication, World Pentecost, was authorized at the
ninth World Pentecostal Fellowship, held in Dallas, Texas,
in 1970. Percy Brewster of Wales was selected to be its
editor. The WPF meets triennially.

2. Pentecostal Fellowship of North America

The PFNA organized in October, 1948, at the urging of the
World Pentecostal Fellowship. The statement of faith is
greatly influenced by the National Association of Evangelicals, an organization in which many of the Pentecostal
bodies hold membership. The statement of faith makes it
impossible for the "Oneness" groups to be included. At
present seventeen denominations participate. The PFNA
meets annually.

3. Society for Pentecostal Studies

SPS conducted its first annual meeting in November, 1971,
at Des Moines, Iowa. The purpose of the Society is to
stimulate and promote Pentecostal Scholarship by providing
a forum for discussion of all academic disciplines in
light of Pentecostal theology. The Pentecostal Fellowship
of North America's statement of faith has been adopted by
the Society, to which full members must subscribe. An
occasional Newsletter is published. The society meets
annually.

4. Full Gospel Business Men's Fellowship International

The organization was started in 1951 under the leadership of
Demos Shakarian, a prominent west coast dairy executive.
The purpose of the organization was to stimulate fellowship
among Pentecostal laymen. FGBMFI has proved to be a major
promotional agency of the Charismatic movement. The statement of faith is similar to that of the Pentecostal Fellowship of North America. The organization publishes a
monthly periodical, Voice. More than 425 local chapters
are presently functioning.

5. Teen Challenge

Though Teen Challenge is not a co-operative effort, it is
listed here as the best example to date of Pentecostals'
involvement in today's social problems. Organized in
1958 by David Wilkerson, a minister for the Assemblies
of God, Teen Challenge is geared to meet head-on the drug
problem of America. There are now twenty-seven Teen
Challenge Centers in major U. S. cities, two in Canada,
and four over seas, in addition to rehabilitation farms
and Bible training centers.[26]

---

26. Christianity Today, 16:43, June 23, 1972.

APPENDIX E

Pentecostal Collections[27]

1. The Oral Roberts University Pentecostal Collection is the most complete. As of January 1, 1972, the collection contained over 7,000 books, 500 periodicals, five legal file sets of pamphlet materials, several hundred tapes and many unpublished theses. Available for purchase are about forty pages of subject bibliographies, in addition to the aforementioned bibliography of periodicals.

2. The Archives of the Pentecostal Holiness Church, located in Franklin Springs, Ga., has an excellent collection of materials relating to the Holiness-Pentecostal groups in the south-east.

3. The Archives of the Church of God at denominational headquarters, Cleveland, Tenn., conatin the best source of documents for the group of denominations known as the Church of God.

4. The Pentecostal File of the Assemblies of God, housed at the headquarters in Springfield, Mo., together with the collections of Central Bible College and Evangel College located in the same city, provide excellent materials on the Keswick groups of Pentecostals.

5. Dr. Walter J. Hollenweger, Department of Theology, University of Birmingham 815, 277, Bimingham 815, 277 England, has the largest private collection on Pentecostalism in the world.

6. David J. DuPlessis, 3742 Linwood Ave., Oakland, Cal., 94602, maintains the best collection of documents relating to the World Pentecostal Fellowship.

7. Hubert Mitchell of Des Moines, Iowa has the best source of Pentecostal Fellowship of North America documents.

---

27. For similar listing of collections relating to Pentecostalism, consult Vinson Synan, The Holiness-Pentecostal Movement, p. 225.

KESWICK:

A BIBLIOGRAPHIC INTRODUCTION

TO

THE HIGHER LIFE MOVEMENTS

111

KESWICK:

A BIBLIOGRAPHIC INTRODUCTION

TO

THE HIGHER LIFE MOVEMENTS

by

David D. Bundy

The Third in a Series of
"Occasional Bibliographic Papers
of the B. L. Fisher Library"

B. L. Fisher Library
Asbury Theological Seminary
Wilmore, Kentucky 40390
1975

Occasional Bibliographic Papers of the
B. L. Fisher Library:

No. 1. The American Holiness Movement; a
        Bibliographic Introduction. Donald
        W. Dayton. 1971. 59 p. $2.00.
        Out-of-print. New edition in process.

No. 2. The American Pentecostal Movement; a
        Bibliographic Essay. David W. Faupel.
        1972. 56 p. $2.00.

No. 3. Keswick: a Bibliographic Introduc-
        tion to the Higher Life Movements.
        David D. Bundy. 1975. 89 p. $3.00.

114

Order Information

Prices listed above for 1 - 10 copies. For
11 or more copies the price per copy is re-
duced by fifty cents ($0.50) plus postage and
handling unless payment accompanies order.

ISBN 0-914368-03-6

Address:

        Director of Library Services
        B. L. Fisher Library
        Asbury Theological Seminary
        Wilmore, Ky. 40390

PREFACE

This third monograph in the series, "Occasional Bibliographic Papers of the B. L. Fisher Library" follows Donald W. Dayton's THE AMERICAN HOLINESS MOVEMENT: A BIBLIOGRAPHIC INTRODUCTION and David W. Faupel's THE AMERICAN PENTECOSTAL MOVEMENT, A BIBLIOGRAPHICAL ESSAY, at the suggestion of Dr. Melvin Dieter.

I wish to express appreciation to Dr. Susan A. Schultz, Director of the B. L. Fisher Library of Asbury Theological Seminary, for her patient encouragement throughout the duration of the project and for her critical evaluation of the manuscript.

A special debt of gratitude is owed to the persons who in responding to the first draft of this essay saved me from a multitiude of errors and provided suggestions from the areas of their expertise: Dr. James Hamilton, Asbury College, has a prodigious knowledge of nineteenth century America and England; Dr. Melvin Dieter* Director of Wesleyan Educational Institutions, and Mr. Donald W. Dayton, Director of Mellander Library and Assistant Professor of Theology at North Park Theological Seminary, are thoroughly aware of the literature and history of the European "Higher Life" Movements and the American Holiness Movement; Mr. David W. Faupel, Assistant Professor of Bibliography and Research at Asbury Theological Seminary has special expertise with regard to the literature of Pentecostalism and has continually provided insights and encouragement during the evolution of this essay; Dr. J. Edwin Orr graciously provided suggestions incorporated herein. I alone accept responsibility for any errors which may remain, and would appreciate information on any inaccuracy discovered by the readers.

I am also grateful for access to several excellent collections and to the unfailing generosity and kind helpfulness of librarians and their staff assistants: Garrett-Evangelical Seminary; Moody Bible Institute; The Southern Baptist Theological Seminary; The Regenstein Library; The University of Chicago; and especially the B. L. Fisher Library, Asbury Theological Seminary. Access to the personal collections of Dr. James Hamilton and Mr. Donald W. Dayton provided materials which filled serious lacunae in my research.

Finally, I wish to express my sincere thanks to Mrs. Joan Smith, Mrs. Wendy Ferns and Mrs. Kris Cryderman who cheerfully and accurately typed from manuscripts that were usually difficult, to Mrs. Gilbert (Esther) James who with patient persistence edited the text and verified bibliographic entries, and to Mrs. Linda Gates who prepared the final copy for printing.

One further word of explanation is due. For historic purposes the publication dates for titles listed are the earliest that could be established, and for brevity's sake, normally, only one publisher is cited. Many of these titles were published on both sides of the Atlantic; many reprints were issued. Please consult both the U. S. and British BOOKS-IN-PRINT for current publication data.

David D. Bundy
Instructor in Greek
Asbury Theological Seminary

* As of September 1, 1975, Dr. Dieter is Associate Professor of Church History, Asbury Theological Seminary.

Contents

INTRODUCTION AND DEFINITION

A difficult problem in attempting to prepare
an introduction to the literature of the Keswick Movement is the matter of definition.
Keswick, a small town in northwest England,
has since 1875 been the site of the famed
Keswick Convention. The Keswick Convention
is not a denomination. It has no membership
rolls. Nor does Keswick have a precisely delimited tradition. The Keswick Convention
is, instead, an amorphous conglomerate of individuals and groups who are in sympathy with
the teachings and lifestyle as taught at the
annual meeting and proclaimed in the official
record of the Keswick Convention, THE KESWICK
WEEK, an annual report of the meeting at Keswick.

The well-known motto of the Convention, founded with the aim of "the promotion of practical holiness," is "All One in Christ Jesus."
Doctrinal and ecclesiastical differences are
minimized for one week each year as evangelical Christians gather to pursue a life of
personal holiness. In classical theological
categories, they strive together for sanctification (progressive) attained by a suppression of sinful desires and tendencies within
individual men.

Keswick, albeit often ignored by church historians, has had an influence during the past
century upon the Christian world far out of
proportion to its humble, faltering beginnings. Its followers have sought to trans-
plant the dynamic of the Keswick Convention,
resulting in "Keswick" camps and conferences
in Canada, India, the United States of America, South Africa, Scotland, Germany, France,
the West Indies, and the Orient. Keswick has
had monumental influence on American Fundamentalism, Pentecostalism, and the American
Holiness Movement.

The method of this essay will be to introduce
the reader to the bibliography of the Keswick
Convention and to indicate sources necessary
for understanding the impact of the Convention around the world. Literature will be
presented around the foci of: (1) History
of Keswick and Its Influence; (2) Resources
for Bibliography; (3) Theological and Biblical Studies; (4) Devotional Literature; (5)
Hymnody; (6) Periodicals; and (7) Historical
Collections. Due to the absence of the usual
denominational or traditional structures, the
history of the Keswick Convention and of its
influence throughout Christendom is the story
of the efforts of and direction given by individuals within the common cause of the higher life. Therefore, a significant portion of
the data provided herein focuses upon the
lives of illustrious men and women.

HISTORY AND INFLUENCE OF KESWICK

Setting the Stage

In order that a more adequate designation and
understanding of this group can occur, a
sketch of the milieus of the origins of the
movement is offered.

The church in England in the middle of the
nineteenth century was plagued with faltering
popular enthusiasm for the religious institutions, accentuated by the rivalry of three
major religious parties. The High Church
party had been recently invigorated by litur-
gical renewal at the impetus of the Oxford
Movement.[1] The Broad Church party sought to

---

1. The Oxford Movement stimulated an immense
   literature. Especially helpful in understanding the movement and its impact are H. P.
Liddon, THE LIFE OF E. B. PUSEY, 4 vols. (London; New York: Longmans, Green, 1893-97);R.W.

revitalize itself on a platform of social reform and by adopting German theological constructs and Darwinian concepts.[2] The Low Church party[3] was strongly influenced by British Methodism, emphasizing the Bible and personal religious experience. Each party strove to improve the church and to influence the church politically in favor of its alternative: all of this under the aegis of Anglicanism.[4] Outside Anglicanism, the Plymouth Brethren and, to some extent, British Methodism offered the alternative of a strict lit-

---

Church, THE OXFORD MOVEMENT. TWELVE YEARS, 1833-1845 (London: Macmillan, 1891); S. Baring-Gould, THE CHURCH REVIVAL (London: Methuen, 1914); S. L. Ollard, A SHORT HISTORY OF THE OXFORD MOVEMENT (London: A. R. Mowbray, 1915). For additional bibliography see F. L. Cross, ed., OXFORD DICTIONARY OF THE CHRISTIAN CHURCH, pp. 1001-1002; James Hastings, ed., ENCYCLOPAEDIA OF RELIGION AND ETHICS, IX, (1917), 585-589.

2. For tendencies of this movement, ESSAYS AND REVIEWS (10th ed.; London: Longman, Green, Longman, & Roberts, 1862); also F. W. Cornish, THE ENGLISH CHURCH IN THE NINETEENTH CENTURY, 2 vols. (London: Macmillan, 1910). For additional study suggestions see OXFORD DICTIONARY OF THE CHRISTIAN CHURCH, p. 199.

3. The Low Church party was commonly termed "Evangelical." See J. H. Overton, THE EVANGELICAL REVIVAL IN THE EIGHTEENTH CENTURY (London: Longmans, Green, 1900), and H. G. C. Moule, THE EVANGELICAL SCHOOL IN THE CHURCH OF ENGLAND (London: J. Nisbet, 1901).

4. The biographical study of the proponents of the various options in the Church of England is of primary interest.

eralistic interpretation of Scripture, a conservative pietistic lifestyle, and a simple faith. But it was the Low Church party and other "evangelicals" from within the Anglican tradition that were to provide the majority of the Keswickians.

A second important factor in the origins of the Keswick Movement was the concern for the higher life, resulting from the overflow of American pietistic revivalism;[5] or, as phrased by Robert S. Fletcher, HISTORY OF OBERLIN COLLEGE (Oberlin: Oberlin College, 1943), "the Oberlinizing of England."[6] Asa

----

5. Although the most immediate stimuli came from America, Keswick apologists trace their heritage in earlier writers. W. H. Griffith Thomas observes in an essay, "The Literature of Keswick," in C. F. Harford's THE KESWICK CONVENTION, ITS MESSAGE, ITS METHOD AND ITS MEN (London: Marshall Brothers, n.d.), p. 223, "... the roots of the distinctive teachings can easily be traced in the writings of Walter Marshall, William Law, John Wesley, Fletcher of Madeley, Thomas à Kempis, Brother Lawrence, Madame Guyon, the letters of Samuel Rutherford and the Memoir of McCheyne." Of Walter Marshall, THE GOSPEL MYSTERY OF SANCTIFICATION (1692), Thomas comments, p. 223, "...[in Marshall], the essential theology of the KESWICK MOVEMENT is clearly seen;..." The Bonars and George Müller were also influential. See also M. E. Dieter, "The Holiness Revival in Nineteenth Century Europe," WESLEYAN THEOLOGICAL JOURNAL 9, (1974), 15-27. See also Dieter, "Revivalism and Holiness," Ph.D. dissertation at Temple University,1973, available in bound copy from University Microfilms, Ann Arbor, Michigan, order number 73-18, 681.

6. Also see the chronicle by a former President of Oberlin College, James H. Fair-

Mahan[7] and Charles Grandison Finney[8] visited
England in 1849 and met with significant successes in evangelistic work, building upon
the impact of their writings, especially Finney's LECTURES ON REVIVALS OF RELIGION (New

---

child, OBERLIN: THE COLONY AND THE COLLEGE
1833-1883 (Oberlin: E. J. Goodrich, 1883).

7. Asa Mahan, like Upham, has been appropri-
    ated by the Holiness, Pentecostal, and
Keswick Movements. See note 15 in Donald W.
Dayton, THE AMERICAN HOLINESS MOVEMENT, A BIB-
LIOGRAPHIC INTRODUCTION. Mr. Dayton in 1973
read papers at both the Wesleyan Theological
Society and the Society of Pentecostal Studies which should soon be available in the organs of the respective societies. Barbara
Zikmund's Duke University Ph.D. dissertation,
"Asa Mahan and Oberlin Perfectionism," available through University Microfilms in hard-
bound copy (University Microfilms order #70-
11, 599), is a good introduction both to the
genius of Mahan and to literature by and
about him.

Mahan's philosophical writings continue to at-
tract attention, especially, A SYSTEM OF IN-
TELLECTUAL PHILOSOPHY (New York: Saxon & Miles,
1845), A CRITICAL HISTORY OF PHILOSOPHY, 2
vols. (New York: Phillips and Hunt, 1883),
and SCIENCE OF MORAL PHILOSOPHY (Oberlin:
Fitch, 1848).

8. Charles Grandison Finney's most signifi-
    cant volume, LECTURES ON REVIVALS OF RELI-
 GION, ed. William G. McLoughlin (Cambridge:
Harvard University Press, 1960), (original
ed. 1835). His MEMOIRS OF CHARLES G. FIN-
NEY (New York: Revell, 1876), have been kept
in print by Revell as THE AUTOBIOGRAPHY OF
CHARLES G. FINNEY. See also Aaron Merritt
Hills, LIFE OF CHARLES G. FINNEY (Cincinnati:
Office of GOD'S REVIVALIST, 1902).

York: Leavitt and Lord, 1835) and Mahan's
SCRIPTURE DOCTRINE OF CHRISTIAN PERFECTION;
WITH OTHER KINDRED SUBJECTS ILLUSTRATED AND
CONFIRMED IN A SERIES OF DISCOURSES DESIGNED
TO THROW LIGHT ON THE WAY OF HOLINESS (Boston:
D. S. King, 1839). Mahan had also received
attention in philosophical circles (see note
7). The Scottish realistic philosophy pio-
neered by Thomas Reid, culminating in the
work of Sir William Hamilton under whom C. G.
Moore and his father studied, provided a foundation which Mahan's perfectionism and Finney's revivalism interpenetrated to undergird
a significant social reform movement. The result of primary interest for this essay is
the influence of the men and their writings
on others who would sensitize the consciousness of the British churches regarding personal holiness; for example, I. E. Page and
John Brash, co-editors of THE KING'S HIGHWAY,
Thornley Smith, Charles Grandison Moore who
edited DIVINE LIFE (British Wesleyan-Holiness),
also LIFE OF FAITH during the later tenure of
Evan Hopkins. Moore, named after Finney, was
a close friend of Mahan and later editor of
his works and executor of his estate. He
continuously added an "Oberlin" perspective
to the Keswickian and Methodist-Holiness periodicals which he edited.

Also influential was the indefatigable James
Caughey.[9] Caughey, who had been closely, as-
sociated with Phoebe Palmer and influenced by
Mahan and Finney, began revivalistic tours in

---

9. In addition to the works cited, HELPS TO
A LIFE OF HOLINESS AND USEFULNESS; OR,
REVIVAL MISCELLANIES, eds. Ralph W. Allen and
Daniel Wise (Boston: J.P. Magee, 1851), and
SHOWERS OF BLESSING FROM CLOUDS OF MERCY; se-
lected from the Journal and other writings of
the Rev. James Caughey (Boston: J. P. Magee,
1857).

England as early as 1841. His successes are
chronicled in THE TRIUMPH OF TRUTH AND CON-
TINENTAL LETTERS AND SKETCHES FROM THE JOUR-
NAL, LETTERS AND SERMONS OF THE REV. JAMES
CAUGHEY WITH AN INTRODUCTION BY JOSEPH CASTLE
(Philadelphia: Higgins and Perkinpine, 1857),
and EARNEST CHRISTIANITY, ILLUSTRATED; OR, SE-
LECTIONS FROM THE JOURNAL OF REV. JAMES CAUGH-
EY WITH A BRIEF SKETCH OF MR. CAUGHEY'S LIFE
by Daniel Wise (Boston: J. P. Magee, 1855).

In addition to the ministry and writings of
these men, the writings of Thomas Upham[10]
and William Arthur[11] were widely circulated.

The revival of 1857-1858 has been described
by Timothy Smith, REVIVALISM AND SOCIAL RE-
FORM (New York: Abingdon, 1957),and by J.
Edwin Orr, THE SECOND EVANGELICAL AWAKENING
IN BRITAIN (London & Edinburgh: Marshall,

---

10. Thomas Upham influenced both the Holi-
    ness Movement in America and Keswick.
His LIFE AND RELIGIOUS OPINIONS AND EXPERI-
ENCES OF MADAME DE LA MOTHE GUYON (N.Y.: Har-
per, 1847), has been frequently reprinted by
H. R. Allenson as LIFE OF MADAME GUYON. PRIN-
CIPLES OF THE INTERIOR OR HIDDEN LIFE (Boston:
D. S. King, 1843), and other works are analyz-
ed by Gregory Peck, "Dr. Upham's Works," METH-
ODIST QUARTERLY REVIEW 28 (1846), 248-265.
See also B. B. Warfield, PERFECTIONISM, II
(New York: Oxford University Press, 1931),
337-459, and Melvin Easterday Dieter, "Revi-
valism and Holiness," chapter 2, pp. 64-68
and notes, 153-164.

11. British Wesleyan-Methodist William Ar-
    thur, TONGUE OF FIRE (London: Hamilton,
Adams, 1856),was widely circulated in American Holiness, Pentecostal and British Keswick
circles; its continued influence is attested
by frequent reprintings.

Morgan and Scott, 1949), and THE SECOND EVAN-
GELICAL AWAKENING IN AMERICA (London: Mar-
shall, Morgan & Scott, 1952). Both of Orr's
books were abridged into a more popular ac-
count, THE SECOND EVANGELICAL AWAKENING, AN
ACCOUNT OF THE SECOND WORLDWIDE EVANGELICAL
REVIVAL BEGINNING IN THE MID NINETEENTH CEN-
TURY (London & Edinburgh: Marshall, Morgan
and Scott, 1955). A portion of the first vol-
ume was printed under the title, AMERICA'S
GREAT REVIVAL (Elizabethtown, Pa.: McBeth
Press, 1957). More accessible is his THE
LIGHT OF THE NATIONS: EVANGELICAL RENEWAL
AND ADVANCE IN THE NINETEENTH CENTURY (Grand
Rapids: Eerdmans, 1965), which is a more gen-
eral discussion of the period.

The message of the American-originated revival was then transported abroad. Mahan re-
turned to England, where he was in continual
demand as a speaker; James Caughey worked in
close cooperation with Phoebe and Dr. W. C.
Palmer whose efforts are detailed in FOUR
YEARS IN THE OLD WORLD; COMPRISING THE TRA-
VELS, INCIDENTS AND EVANGELISTIC LABORS OF
DR. AND MRS. PALMER IN ENGLAND, IRELAND, SCOT-
LAND AND WALES (New York: Foster and Palmer,
1866). Finney undertook another tour of the
British Isles. The dramatic results have
been ably chronicled by Orr.

During the two decades following the English
revivals of 1858-1859 holiness conventions
were going on all over England. Mahan,
through his involvement in the pre-Keswick
conferences discussed below and his editorship of DIVINE LIFE, helped to unify the higher life aspirations arising from the "Oberlinizing of England" and to focus them in the
direction of the Wesleyan-Holiness theological
heritage combined with an emphasis on the baptism of the Holy Spirit. Thus, the ground-
work was laid for the visits of the Moody-
Sankey team, the Robert Pearsall Smiths and
William Edwin Boardman to England, France

and Germany.[12]

---

12. William Edwin Boardman, a product of the
     "Burned-Over District" of New York and
a graduate of Lane Theological Seminary, Cincinnati, was a controversial promoter of the
higher life. Closely related to the American
Holiness Movement, his very influential book,
THE HIGHER CHRISTIAN LIFE (Boston: Henry
Hoyt, 1859, revised 1871), argued that every
Christian must achieve a higher plane of
Christian life, entered by an act of faith as
at justification. His theological perspective is critiqued by Jacob J. Abbott, "Boardman's Higher Christian Life," BIBLIOTHECA
SACRA AND BIBLICAL REPOSITORY, 17 (July 1860),
508-535; by John A. Todd, "Law of Spiritual
Growth," THE BIBLICAL REPERTORY AND PRINCE-
TON REVIEW, 32 (1860), 608-640. Both of
these reviewers take Boardman to task for
faulty scholarship and theological error.
Boardman's work is also evaluated by Warfield, PERFECTIONISM, II, 463-494. The most
severe critique is that of Henry A. Boardman,
"THE HIGHER LIFE" DOCTRINE OF SANCTIFICATION
TRIED BY THE WORD OF GOD (Philadelphia: Presbyterian Board of Publication, 1877), which
serves to evaluate the entire resultant movement. A less influential work was IN THE POW-
ER OF THE SPIRIT; OR, CHRISTIAN EXPERIENCE IN
THE LIGHT OF THE BIBLE (London: Daldy, Isbister, 1875). Despite the obvious shortcomings
of his work, Boardman, perhaps more than any-
one else, raised interest in the possibility
of the higher Christian life. His life has
been chronicled by his wife, THE LIFE AND LA-
BORS OF THE REV. W. E. BOARDMAN (New York:
Appleton, 1887). It is enthusiastic and at
times self-contradictory but no more adequate
work has been produced.

W. E. Boardman, THE HIGHER CHRISTIAN LIFE
(Boston: Henry Hoyt, 1858), is credited by

In 1872 Mr. & Mrs. Robert Pearsall Smith,[13] Quakers from the American Holiness Movement, sought respite in England from their American religious and mercantile labors. They

---

Steven Barabas, SO GREAT SALVATION, THE HISTORY AND MESSAGE OF THE KESWICK MOVEMENT (Westwood, N. J.: Revell, 1952), p. 16, as being the most influential in arousing interest in sanctification and the Spirit-filled life.

In addition to Mahan, Boardman, and Arthur, the writings of Richard Poole, CENTER AND CIRCLE OF EVANGELICAL RELIGION; OR, PERFECT LIFE (London: Jarrold, 1873),and Hannah Whitall Smith, THE CHRISTIAN'S SECRET OF A HAPPY LIFE (New York: Revell, 1875),had wide and influential circulation; as did the writings of George Müller,NARRATIVE OF THE LORD'S DEALINGS WITH GEORGE MÜLLER, (London: Nisbet, 1895),1st ed., 1837 and in later American editions, THE LIFE OF TRUST: with an introduction by Francis Wayland. THE DIARY OF GEORGE MÜLLER, (London: Pickering & Inglis, 1954),was edited by A. Rendle Short. There are biographies by W. H. Harding, THE LIFE OF GEORGE MÜLLER, A RECORD OF FAITH TRIUMPHANT (London: Morgan & Scott, 1914), Basil W. Miller, GEORGE MÜLLER, THE MAN OF FAITH; A BIOGRAPHY OF ONE OF THE GREATEST PRAYER-WARRIORS OF THE PAST CENTURY (Grand Rapids: Zondervan, 1951), and the often reprinted work of A. T. Pierson, GEORGE MÜLLER OF BRISTOL AND HIS WITNESS TO A PRAYER-HEARING GOD (New York: Baker and Taylor, 1899), containing a preface by Müller's son-in-law, James Wright.

13. Robert Pearsall Smith has not been the subject of any extensive critical biography. Some details may be gleaned from the writings of his wife, Hannah Whitall Smith, and their son, Logan Pearsall Smith,

were soon involved in meetings of select groups in private homes, and in 1873, togeth-

---

but most of his life remains shrouded from view. Most helpful are Logan Pearsall Smith, UNFORGOTTEN YEARS (Boston: Little, Brown, 1939); Hannah Whitall Smith; THE RECORD OF A HAPPY LIFE: BEING MEMORIALS OF FRANKLIN WHIT-ALL SMITH (Philadelphia, Privately printed, 1873); "Smith, Robert Pearsall," DIE RELIGION IN GESCHICHTE UND GEGENWART, VI 1962 (3rd ed.; Tübingen: Mohr),112; "The Religious Experience of R. Pearsall Smith," THE CHRISTIAN OB-SERVER 75 (1875, London), 830 ff., 926 ff.; 76 (1876), 60 ff. Also available but less biographical are Fr. Winkler, "Robert Pearsall Smith und der Perfectionismus" in Friedrich D. Kropatscheck, BIBLISCHE ZEIT UND STREITFRAGEN ZUR AUFKLÄRUNG DER GEBILDETEN Series 10 (Berlin-Lichterfielde: Edwin Runge, 1914), 410-422 and Johannes Jüngst, AMERI-KANISCHER METHODISMUS IN DEUTSCHLAND UND RO-BERT PEARSALL SMITH (Gotha, F. A. Perthes, 1875). See also B. B. Warfield, PERFECTION-ISM, II (New York: Oxford University Press, 1931),and M. E. Dieter, "Revivalism and Holiness." The Cowper-Temple Correspondence, Broadlands Archives has material relating primarily to the period of the Broadlands Conference.

His own writings were very influential in provoking interest in the higher life in England. HOLINESS THROUGH FAITH; LIGHT ON THE WAY OF HOLINESS (London: Morgan and Scott, 1870), "WALK IN THE LIGHT." WORDS OF COUNSEL TO THOSE WHO HAVE ENTERED INTO "THE REST OF FAITH" (London: n.p.,1873), had a lasting influence. As editor of THE CHRISTIAN'S PATH-WAY TO POWER he influenced the revival movements of America and England. An extensive listing of Smith's writings is found in Warfield, PERFECTIONISM, II, 510.

er with W. E. Boardman they held a series of breakfasts focusing on the subject of the higher life. This served as a prelude to three conferences or conventions which, in turn, spawned the Keswick Convention.

The support of W. Cowper-Temple (later Lord Mount Temple),made possible the Conference of July 17-23, 1874 on his Broadlands estate.[14] One hundred attended, including George Macdonald, Theodore Monod,[15] Mrs. Amanda Smith,[16]

---

14. Material relevant to the Broadlands Convention may be found in the Cowper-Temple Correspondence at the Broadlands Archives; in Edna Jackson, THE LIFE THAT IS LIFE INDEED: REMEMBRANCES OF THE BROADLANDS CONFERENCES (London: Nisbet, 1910), and in most histories of the KESWICK MOVEMENT.

15. Theodore Monod, a pastor in Paris, influenced by Robert Pearsall Smith, was a well known figure in British higher life meetings. His books and tracts are still being reprinted, primarily by "Back to the Bible Broadcast," Box 82808, Lincoln, Nebraska 68501. LOOKING UNTO JESUS (Lincoln: BBB, 1973), 22 pps., contains a note indicating 625,000 copies of this tract have been published. THE GIFT OF LIFE (London: Morgan & Scott, 1912), THE GIFT OF GOD (London: Morgan & Scott, 1876), and DENYING SELF, ed. H. F. Bowker (London: Frome, 1878), and LIFE MORE ABUNDANT (London: Morgan & Scott, 1881),are all books of addresses delivered at higher life conferences, primarily at Keswick. No biographical material has been found, nor is there a comprehensive list of Monod's works. He was the author of the famous Keswick song, "None of Self and All of Thee."

16. Mrs. Amanda Smith, a former slave with little formal education, traveled through-

the Black holiness evangelist, and Canon Wilberforce. Robert Pearsall Smith was the chairman. Out of the concern that this type of conference be more widely available, the Oxford Convention,[17] August 29-September 7, 1874, featured Robert Pearsall Smith as chairman and principal speaker. His wife, Hannah Whitall Smith,[18] Theodore Monod, Evan H.

---

out the world "representing" the American Holiness Movement. Her AUTOBIOGRAPHY; THE STORY OF THE LORD'S DEALING WITH MRS. AMANDA SMITH, THE COLORED EVANGELIST, was published in 1893 by Meyer & Bro. of Chicago and recently reprinted (Noblesville, Ind.: J. Edwin Newby, 1962). See also, M. H. Cadbury, THE LIFE OF AMANDA SMITH, "THE AFRICAN SYBIL, THE CHRISTIAN SAINT," with an introduction by J. Rendel Harris (Birmingham, England: Cornish Bros., 1916), and Marshall William Taylor, THE LIFE, TRAVELS, LABORS, AND HELPERS OF MRS. AMANDA SMITH, THE FAMOUS NEGRO MISSIONARY EVANGELIST (Cincinnati: Cranston and Stowe, 1886).

17. ACCOUNT OF THE UNION MEETING FOR THE PRO-
    MOTION OF SCRIPTURAL HOLINESS, HELD AT OXFORD, August 29th to September 7th, 1874 (Chicago: Revell, 1874), is a rather wordy but detailed account of the proceedings. See also ADVOCATE OF CHRISTIAN HOLINESS 5 (1874), 134-135 and THE METHODIST MAGAZINE 17 (1874), 992-997. These and other Holiness Movement and/or Methodist periodicals carried enthusiastic reports of the convention.

18. Hannah Whitall Smith, as with her hus-
    band Robert Pearsall Smith, (see above) has not been the subject of critical biographies. She gives an account of their early religious experiences in THE RECORD OF A HAPPY LIFE: BEING MEMORIALS OF FRANKLIN WHITALL SMITH (Philadelphia: Lippincott, 1873), and of her own pilgrimage in THE UN-

Hopkins,[19] Asa Mahan, and W. E. Boardman also
spoke.

SELFISHNESS OF GOD, AND HOW I DISCOVERED IT
(London: J. Nisbet, 1903); the American edi-
tion, THE UNSELFISHNESS OF GOD, AND HOW I DIS-
COVERED IT; A SPIRITUAL AUTOBIOGRAPHY (N.Y.:
Revell, 1903).

Her granddaughter, Ray Strachey (Rachel Cos-
telloe), A QUAKER GRANDMOTHER (N.Y.: Revell,
1914), chronicles her last years, and in RELI-
GIOUS FANATICISM; EXTRACTS FROM THE PAPERS OF
HANNAH WHITALL SMITH (London: Faber & Gwyer,
1928),presents aspects of her religious experiences. Logan Pearsall Smith, her son, published his reminiscences in UNFORGOTTEN YEARS
(Boston: Little, Brown, 1939),and her letters
in A RELIGIOUS REBEL: THE LETTERS OF "H.W.S."
(London: Nisbet, 1949),with a biographical
preface by Robert Gathorne-Hardy.[American edition: PHILADELPHIA QUAKER; THE LETTERS OF HAN-
NAH WHITALL SMITH (N.Y.: Harcourt,Brace,1950]).

132

Mrs. Smith was a very influential writer, far
surpassing her husband. THE CHRISTIAN'S SE-
CRET OF A HAPPY LIFE (N.Y.: Revell, 1875),orig-
inally published in her husband's periodical THE CHRISTIAN'S PATHWAY TO POWER, has been
continuously reprinted and translated. Also
important are: BIBLE READINGS ON THE PROGRES-
SIVE DEVELOPMENT OF TRUTH AND EXPERIENCE IN
THE O.T. SCRIPTURES (London: Elliot Stock,
1878), BIBLE STUDIES ON THE HIGHER LIFE (London: Longley, 1891), THE VEIL UPLIFTED; OR,
THE BIBLE ITS OWN INTERPRETER (London: Longley, 1886), LIVING IN THE SUNSHINE (N.Y.: Revell, 1906), published also as THE GOD OF ALL
COMFORT (London: Nisbet, 1906), THE INTERIOR
LIFE (London: Longley, 1886), and EVERY-DAY
RELIGION; OR, THE COMMON-SENSE TEACHING OF
THE BIBLE (N.Y.: Revell, 1893).

19. Evan Henry Hopkins (1837-1918), for many
years the leader of Keswick and the chief

The Brighton Convention,[20] May 29-June 7,
1875, again with Smith as chairman, featured
speakers of later Keswick fame: E. H. Hopkins, Stevenson A. Blackwood, H. W. Webb-Peploe and Theodore Monod. An exciting success,
cheered on by Moody, it was the Smiths' last
convention in England. The stage was set for
the Keswick Convention.

---

guide in matters of doctrine, is the subject
of a study by his friend, Alexander Smellie,
EVAN HENRY HOPKINS. A MEMOIR (London: Mar-
shall Bros., 1920), and in an introductory
appreciation by Fred Mitchell in a reprint of
Hopkins' most influential book, THE LAW OF
LIBERTY IN THE SPIRITUAL LIFE (Philadelphia:
The Sunday School Times, 1952). The first
edition was published in London in 1884 by
Marshall Brothers. Other significant works
by Hopkins are BROKEN BREAD FOR DAILY USE,
BEING THOUGHTS AND COMMENTS ON THE HEADLINE
TEXTS OF "DAILY LIGHT ON THE DAILY PATH" (Lon-
don: Samuel Bagster, 1895), HIDDEN YET POS-
SESSED (London: Marshall Bros., 1894), TALKS
WITH BEGINNERS IN THE DIVINE LIFE (London:
Marshall Bros., 1909), THOUGHTS ON LIFE AND
GODLINESS (London: Hodder & Stoughton, 1878),
and THE WALK THAT PLEASES GOD (London: Mar-
shall Bros., 1887).

20. RECORD OF THE CONVENTION FOR THE PROMO-
     TION OF SCRIPTURAL HOLINESS HELD AT
BRIGHTON, May 29th to June 7th, 1875 (Brighton:
W. J. Smith, 1875), is a detailed account of
the meetings, messages, and responses. Nearly eight thousand people attended the Convention including participants from France and
Germany. The emphasis as recorded, is on the
internal experience; little social concern is
reflected, which a few decades before had
been the heart cry of the American Holiness
Movement which provided the impetus for Brighton. Indicative is the favorite hymn of the

The Reverend T. D. H. Battersby,[21] who attended the Oxford Convention, and a friend, Robert Wilson, initiated the first Keswick Convention and scheduled it to begin three weeks
after the Brighton Convention. It was to be
chaired by Smith, but he cancelled due to reasons still obscure, leaving Battersby support-
ed by speakers Webb-Peploe, George R. Thornton, T. Phillips, H. F. Bowker, T. M. Croome
and Murray Shipley to lead the circa 400 in

Convention, "Jesus Saves Me Now." Brighton
was middle class in expression and in values.
The entire movement therefore tended to be
more "quietistic" than the American Holiness
Movement. This is true, relatively, even today.

134

21. Canon Thomas Dundas Harford Battersby
     may be called the founder of the Kes-
wick Convention. An Oxford graduate who had
gone from High Church to Broad Church, he attended Oxford and Brighton, experiencing
"resting faith." His sons wrote an apology
for his life and beliefs, MEMOIR OF T. D.
HARFORD-BATTERSBY, LATE VICAR OF ST. JOHN'S,
KESWICK. . .TOGETHER WITH SOME ACCOUNT OF THE
KESWICK CONVENTION. With a preface by H. C.
G. Moule (London: Seeley, 1890). Battersby
wrote and published several sermons on the
holy life, CHRIST IN THE HEART (London:
Wertheim, 1860), HIGHER ATTAINMENTS IN CHRIS-
TIAN HOLINESS, AND HOW TO PROMOTE THEM (Lon-
don: Nisbet, 1875). In 1878 he published
BONDAGE OR LIBERTY? A SKETCH OF ST. PAUL'S
TEACHING IN ROMANS VI-VIII (London: Hodder &
Stoughton), a doctrinal apologetic for a Kes-
wickian understanding of original sin, justi-
fication and sanctification. Battersby edit-
ed REMINISCENCES OF THE KESWICK CONVENTION
(London: Partridge, 1879), discussed above.

attendance into the higher Christian life.
The first meeting has been the focal point of
several histories of the movement. Evan Hopkins, "Preliminary Stages" and Webb-Peploe
and E. W. Moore, "Early Keswick Conventions,"
chapters in THE KESWICK CONVENTION, ITS MES-
SAGE, ITS METHOD AND ITS MEN (London: Marshall Bros., 1907),are accounts by participants, as are E. H. Hopkins, THE STORY OF KES-
WICK, Eighteenth Convention, 1892 (London:
Life of Faith, 1892), and THE KESWICK JUBILEE
SOUVENIR, THE STORY OF THE CONVENTION'S FIFTY
YEARS' MINISTRY AND INFLUENCE (London: Marshall Bros., 1925). These are short, popular,
and enthusiastically uncritical. Walter B.
Sloan, THESE SIXTY YEARS, THE STORY OF THE
KESWICK CONVENTION (London: Pickering and Inglis, n.d.,1935?),is a chronicle of the movement. Tedious in laborious detail, it plods
through the years reading rather like minutes
kept for business sessions. There are good
photographs of the most influential men of
the movement, but not a solitary bibliographic   clue appears to lead the reader to his
sources. Arthur Tappan Pierson,[22] THE KES-
WICK MOVEMENT, ITS PRECEPT AND PRACTICE,
with introduction by Rev. Evan H. Hopkins
(New York & London: Funk & Wagnalls, 1903)is
an apologetic history of the movement and an
effort to present the movement's theological

135

----

22. ARTHUR TAPPAN PIERSON, A SPIRITUAL WAR-
     RIOR, MIGHTY IN THE SCRIPTURES; A LEADER
IN THE MODERN MISSIONARY CRUSADE (New York:
Revell, 1912), is by his son, Delavan Leonard
Pierson. An able apologist for the Keswick
distinctives, A. T. P. wrote THE KESWICK MOVE-
MENT IN PRECEPT AND PRACTICE (New York: Funk
& Wagnalls, 1903), and FORWARD MOVEMENTS OF
THE LAST HALF CENTURY (New York: Funk & Wag-
nalls, 1900). Many of his works are listed
in Jones, A GUIDE TO THE STUDY OF THE HOLI-
NESS MOVEMENT.

foci. It is written carefully in popular style.

Battersby, REMINISCENCES OF THE KESWICK CONVENTION, 1879, WITH ADDRESSES BY PASTOR OTTO STOCKMAYER (London: S. W. Partridge, 1879), is a valuable bit of data (40 pp.). Of primary importance but hard to find and consequently ignored is Battersby, MEMOIR OF T. D. HARFORD BATTERSBY TOGETHER WITH SOME ACCOUNTS OF THE KESWICK CONVENTION, by two of his sons with a preface by H. C. G. Moule (London: Seeley, 1890). Evan H. Hopkins, that grand patriarch of the first decades, left his memoirs, A STANDARD BEARER OF FAITH AND HOLINESS; REMINISCENCES WITH A MEMOIR BY THE AUTHOR (London: Morgan and Scott, 1919). It is of little scientific value but its 47 pages provide one view of the beginnings.

From this same era comes J.B. Figgis, KESWICK FROM WITHIN (London: Marshall Bros., 1914), an indispensable but less than fluid commentary on the conventions. Figgis is an apologist for the movement as is the American professor at Crozer Theological Seminary, E. H. Johnson, THE HIGHEST LIFE, A STORY OF SHORTCOMINGS AND A GOAL; INCLUDING A FRIENDLY ANALYSIS OF THE KESWICK MOVEMENT (New York: A. C. Armstrong, 1901),which is not as friendly as the title would lead one to suspect. The British version of Keswick is given a higher rating than are the modifications of Moody at Northfield.

Steven Barabas, SO GREAT SALVATION, THE HISTORY AND MESSAGE OF THE KESWICK CONVENTION (Westwood, N. J.: Revell, 1952; London: Marshall, Morgan & Scott, 1952),with a preface by Fred Mitchell, Chairman of the Keswick Convention Council 1948-1951, is still the standard history of the movement. It contains a sketch of the beginnings of the convention, an exposition of Keswickian teaching, biographical sketches of some Keswick leaders

and the most extensive bibliography of material related to Keswick and to the men of the
movement. J. C. Pollock, THE KESWICK STORY,
THE AUTHORIZED HISTORY OF THE KESWICK CONVEN-
TION (London: Hodder & Stoughton, 1964), is
an attempt to popularize the history of the
movement. The result is much more concern
with dramatic effect than with the facts. It
is of little scholarly value having neither
documentation, bibliography nor concern for
critical historical methodology. It is, however, the only chronicle of the World War II
era and after, when Keswick was preoccupied
with theology rather than history (see below,
Theology and Biblical Studies).

Those outside the Keswick Convention made only limited efforts to analyze and understand
the genius of Keswick. B. B. Warfield, PER-
FECTIONISM, 2 vols. (New York: Oxford University Press, 1931), gives considerable space to
a critique of the early influences on the
movement. He is very critical of their concerns. PERFECTIONISM has been reissued in a
one volume edition (Presbyterian and Reformed,
1958),with the material on Thomas Upham de-
leted. More helpful and without the flaming
prejudice of Warfield is the superb work of
Melvin Easterday Dieter "Revivalism and Holiness" (see above note 5), Temple University
Ph.D. dissertation, 1973, University Microfilms Order Number 73-18, 681. His article,
"From Vineland and Menheim to Brighton and
Berlin: The Holiness Revival in Nineteenth-
Century Europe," WESLEYAN THEOLOGICAL JOURNAL
9 (1974), 15-27, draws heavily upon the dissertation, and is a sober, responsible analysis of the background of Keswick.

Finally, Herbert F. Stevenson, editor of LIFE
OF FAITH has prepared a series of supplements
to that periodical featuring the history of
LIFE OF FAITH, formerly THE CHRISTIAN'S PATH-
WAY TO POWER founded by Robert Pearsall Smith
and later edited by William E. Boardman,

Charles G. Moore[23] and Evan H. Hopkins, and
J. K. Maclean. As the closest, although independent, organ of the Keswick Movement, a
study of its history quite naturally shed
light on Keswick.

Influence of Keswick

The Welsh Revival. A fascinating problem of
nationalism and of historiography is the rela-
tionship of the Keswick Convention to the
Welsh Revival. Mrs. Jessie Penn-Lewis, THE
AWAKENING IN WALES AND SOME OF THE HIDDEN
SPRINGS...WITH AN INTRODUCTION TO THE WELSH
REVIVALS BY J. CYNDDYLAN JONES (London: Marshall Bros., 1905), indicates that the roots
of the revival in Wales were to be found in
Keswick. The same approach is taken by Rhyc
Bevan Jones, RENT HEAVENS, THE REVIVAL OF
1904, SOME OF ITS HIDDEN SPRINGS AND PROMI-
NENT RESULTS (London: S. Martin, 1931). However, the assertion of dependency when voiced
by F. B. Meyer provoked a running newspaper
battle and eventual rejection of the Welsh Revival by Keswick.[24] For additional detail

138

---

23. Charles Grandison Moore was de facto ed-
    itor during the tenure of Evan Hopkins.
It was important to the early leaders that
close ties be maintained with the Anglican
Church, and Moore was a Methodist. He contributed a volume to the Keswick Library, 11,
"THINGS WHICH CANNOT BE SHAKEN" (London: Marshall Bros., 1894), and abridged the autobiography of Amanda Smith for British readers.

24. See A. T. Pierson, "The Revival in Wales,"
    EXPERIENCE, (July-Sept., 1905), pp. 94-97.
He suggests that the revival had its origin
in a "prayer-circle" formed at Keswick, 1902,
consisting of Pierson, Moore, Albert Head and
F. Paynter. The revival was compared to that
of 1859 and heralded as "the beginning of the
latter rain."

and references to articles, see Eifion Evans, THE WELSH REVIVAL OF 1904 (Port Talbot, Glamorgan: Evangelical Movement of Wales, 1969), the best analysis of the revival. J. C. Pollock, THE KESWICK STORY (London: Hodder & Stoughton, 1964),gives the Keswick Convention's perspective on the interaction. Accounts by participants and onlookers include John Vyrnwy Morgan, THE WELSH REVIVAL, 1904-5, A RETROSPECT AND A CRITICISM (London: Chapman & Hall, 1909),who takes the phenomenon to task for its lack of tangible results beyond the rhetoric. David Matthews, I SAW THE WELSH REVIVAL (Chicago: Moody Press, 1957),is more popular, but helpful. J. Edwin Orr, THE FLAMING TONGUE, THE IMPACT OF THE TWENTIETH CENTURY REVIVALS (Chicago: Moody Press, 1973),seeks to measure the influence of the Welsh Revival, indicating its significance for understanding the Pentecostal Movement in America. An account of the Welsh Revival by the American Holiness leader, S. B. Shaw, THE GREAT REVIVAL IN WALES, ALSO AN ACCOUNT OF THE GREAT REVIVAL IN IRELAND IN 1859 (Chicago: S. B. Shaw, 1906),includes reports by Mrs. M. Baxter, F. B. Meyers and R. A. Torrey. The book figured prominently in the Azusa Street revivals, being widely read by the participants.

The life of Evan Roberts, whose meteoric rise and demise encompassed the greatest portion of this revival, has been chronicled by D. M. Phillips, EVAN ROBERTS, THE GREAT WELSH REVIVALIST AND HIS WORD, 3rd ed. (London: Marshall Bros., 1906). This is a tedious, enthusiastic reiteration of the bulk of Roberts' revivalistic efforts. A considerable quantity of correspondence is printed here. Mrs. Jessie Penn-Lewis, who cared for Roberts after his withdrawal from ministry (due, it is supposed, to a mental breakdown) became the leader of the continuing revival movement. In collaboration with Roberts, she wrote WAR ON THE SAINTS, A TEXTBOOK FOR BELIEVERS ON THE WORK

OF DECEIVING-SPIRITS AMONG THE CHILDREN OF GOD (London: Marshall Bros., 1912). She founded the OVERCOMER, a deeper life periodical, and served for several years as its editor. Her memoirs were published by Mary N. Garrard, MRS. PENN-LEWIS: A MEMOIR, COMPILED LARGELY FROM MRS. PENN-LEWIS' DIARIES AND NOTES (London: Overcomer Book Room, 1931).

The German Holiness Movement. Between the Oxford and Brighton conventions, Robert Pearsall Smith made a well received tour-crusade through Germany sponsored by the Free Churches. The literature on this tour and its results in German ecclesiastical history is fragmentary. The best English language summary of the Holiness Revival in Germany is in Melvin E. Dieter's, "Revivalism and Holiness," chapter IV (see note, 5).

The most prolific historian of the German Holiness Movement is Paul Fleisch, whose DIE HEILIGUNGSBEWEGUNG VON WESLEY BIS BOARDMAN, VOL. 1 of ZUR GESCHICHTE DER HEILIGUNGSBEWEGUNG, Erstes Heft (Leipzig: H. G. Wallman, 1910), must be the starting point of any future study. Emphasizing Boardman, he also discusses Oberlin theology as represented by Finney and Mahan. The theology of Thomas Upham and R. P. Smith are also treated. Two of his articles, "Der Heiligungslehre der Oxforder Bewegung" NEUE KIRCHLICHE ZEITSCHRIFT 35 (1924), 49-87 and "Die Entstehung der deutschen Heiligungsbewegung vor 50 Jahren," NEUE KIRCHLICHE ZEITSCHRIFT 38 (1927), 663-702 trace the influence of Smith, and the Brighton and Oxford meetings. Fleisch's articles in DIE RELIGION IN GESCHICHTE UND GEGENWART, 2nd ed., on Mahan, Finney, Smith and various other holiness leaders and themes are significant.

Smith's efforts are summarized in Fr. Winkler, "Robert Pearsall Smith und der Perfectionismus," BIBLISCHE ZEIT- UND STREITFRAGEN ZUR AUFKLÄRUNG DES GEBILDETEN 9 (1914), 401-422

and by B. B. Warfield, PERFECTIONISM, II,
503 ff. On German Methodism, see H. Branden-
burg, "Heiligungsbewegung," DIE RELIGION IN
GESCHICHTE UND GEGENWART, III (3rd ed.; Tü-
bingen: Mohr, 1959), 182, Paul F. Douglass,
THE STORY OF GERMAN METHODISM: BIOGRAPHY OF
AN IMMIGRANT SOUL (New York: Methodist Book
Concern, 1939), and A. L. Drummond, GERMAN
PROTESTANTISM SINCE LUTHER (London: Epworth
Pr., 1951).

The movement in Germany which resulted from
the holiness revival has been chronicled by
A. L. Drummond, H. Brandenburg, and Paul F.
Douglass as well as L. Tiesmayer, "Was jeder-
man von der christlichen Gemeinschaftsbewe-
gung in Deutschland wissen muss," DIE RELI-
GION IN GESCHICHTE UND GEGENWART, II (2nd ed.;
Tübingen: Mohr, 1928), 1751-1752, which in-
cludes significant bibliography. Adbel R.
Wentz, GERMANY'S MODERN PIETISTIC MOVEMENT
(n.p.: n.n., n.d.),is excellent as is P.
Fleisch, DIE MODERNE GEMEINSCHAFTBEWEGUNG
IN DEUTSCHLAND: EIN VERSUCH, DIESELBE NACH
IHREN URSPRUENGEN DARZUSTELLEN UND ZU WÜR-
DIGEN (Leipzig: H. G. Wallman, 1903).

Theodor Jellinghaus, Otto Stockmayer and Hein-
rich Rappard were the most influential theo-
logians of the movement. They and others are
featured in Ernst Modersohn, MEN OF REVIVAL
IN GERMANY (Frankfort am Main: Harold Pub.,
n.d.), a popular exposition of the lives of
these men. Otto Stockmayer was often on the
platform at Keswick, and his SANCTIFIED ONES
(New York: n.n., 1904?), had at least two e-
ditions. Important in Switzerland and Germany
were DIE GNADE IST ERSCHIENEN (München: Ank-
er, 1949), ABRAHAM, DER VATER DER GLÄUBIGEN
(Basel: Brunnen, 1943), and DIE GABE DES
HEILIGEN GEISTES (Basel: n.n., 1898). See
also J. C. Pollock, THE KESWICK STORY, passim,
and DIE RELIGION IN GESCHICHTE UND GEGENWART,
VI (3rd ed.; Tübingen: Mohr, 1962), 386, regarding Stockmayer's life and influence. Sev-

eral of Stockmayer's addresses were edited
by T. D. H. Battersby, REMINISCENCES OF THE
KESWICK CONVENTION, ADDRESSES OF PASTOR STOCK-
MAYER AT THE KESWICK CONVENTION (London: S.
W. Partridge, 1879),and in Stockmayer's, THE
BODY OF CHRIST AND ITS DIVINE ARCHITECT (Lon-
don: J. Snow, 1899).

Theodor Jellinghaus, though less well known
in England and America, was a missionary, pastor, theologian, and biblical expositor, DER
BRIEF PAULI AN DIE RÖMER (Auslegung des Neuen
Testaments, 6, Berlin: Thormann & Goetsch,
1903).   His DAS VOLLIGE, GEGENWARTIGE HEIL
DURCH CHRISTUM (Berlin: Prochnow, 1880; 4th
ed. Basel: Kober, Spittlers, 1898), outlined
a rather "Keswickian" understanding of holiness, avoiding the "perfectionist" persuasion
of American Methodism.   PHILADELPHIA, a periodical published by the Committee for the Cul-
tivation of Christian Fellowship and Evangelical Piety, was edited with considerable success by Jellinghaus and served as a cohesive
element for the rapidly growing movement.

142

Foreign Missions.   The Keswick Convention has
been an influential force in Christian missions, not so much in terms of direct personal support as in the inspiring of persons to
enter foreign missionary service and in motivating the wealthier churchmen of Britain to
promote and provide for missions.   For material relating to this concern see John Pollock,
"Keswick Convention," in CONCISE DICTIONARY
OF THE CHRISTIAN WORLD MISSION, ed. Stephen
Neill (Nashville: Abingdon, 1971), p. 322.
More helpful is the well-indexed HISTORY OF
THE CHURCH MISSIONARY SOCIETY: ITS ENVIRON-
MENT, ITS MEN AND ITS WORK, by Eugene Stock,
Vol. III (London: Church Missionary Society,
1899).   This volume is a gold mine of data regarding the development of missionary concern
within the Convention leading to the"Mission-
ary Meetings," under the leadership of Regi-
nald Radcliffe, and to the eventual sending

of Convention missionaries. The first of
these was Amy Carmichael, whose story has
been told by Frank Houghton, AMY CARMICHAEL
OF DOHNAVUR: THE STORY OF A LOVER AND HER
BELOVED (London: S.P.C.K., 1953).

James Hudson Taylor was a key figure in Keswick missions. The China Inland Mission,
which he founded, had many contacts with the
Convention and drew support from it. Taylor's
principal biographers were his son and daughter-in-law, Dr. and Mrs. (Frederick) Howard
Taylor. J. HUDSON TAYLOR, FOUNDER OF THE CHI-
NA INLAND MISSION (Chicago: Moody, 1965),
was abridged by Phyllis Thompson from the
earlier two volume life, HUDSON TAYLOR IN
EARLY YEARS: THE GROWTH OF A SOUL and HUDSON
TAYLOR AND THE CHINA INLAND MISSION: THE
GROWTH OF A WORK OF GOD (London: Morgan &
Scott, 1911-1918), both of which have gone
through several editions. The Howard Taylors
also wrote HUDSON TAYLOR'S SPIRITUAL SECRET   **143**
(London: China Inland Mission, 1932). More
popular are Marshall Broomhall, HUDSON TAYLOR,
THE MAN WHO BELIEVED GOD(London: China In-
land Mission, 1929), and J. C. Pollock, HUDSON
TAYLOR AND MARIA: PIONEERS IN CHINA (London:
Hodder & Stoughton, 1962). Important is M.
Geraldine Guinness, (Mrs. F. H. Taylor) THE
STORY OF THE CHINA INLAND MISSION, 2 vols.
(London: Morgan & Scott, 1893-94).

From Taylor's own hand are A RETROSPECT (London: Morgan, 1894), and UNION AND COMMUNION:
OR THOUGHTS ON THE SONG OF SOLOMON (London:
Morgan & Scott, 1894), the latter first
printed in CHINA'S MILLIONS. The 1914 edition contains a foreword by J. Stuart Holden.

C. G. Moore was with Taylor in China before
being forced to return to England by his
wife's illness. He then became the unidenti-
fied editor of LIFE OF FAITH and was thereby
responsible for the increased mission focus
of the periodical. Fred Mitchell, for some

time Home Director of The China Inland Mission, became chairperson of the Keswick Convention. Mitchell's biographer is Phyllis Thompson, CLIMBING ON TRACK: A BIOGRAPHY OF FRED MITCHELL (London: China Inland Mission, 1953).

Other accounts by men involved in the first beginnings of missionary awareness at Keswick were contributed to THE KESWICK CONVENTION, edited by Charles F. Harford (London: Marshall Bros., 1907). Eugene Stock contributed an essay entitled, "The Missionary Element," J. H. Battersby, "The Keswick Mission Council," and F. B. Meyer and Charles Inwood, "In Other Lands," the latter being a record of tours by Keswick speakers to lend spiritual and emotional support to missionaries on the field. Steven Barabas, SO GREAT SALVATION, is a significant source. See also John Pollock, THE KESWICK STORY (London: Hodder & Stoughton, 1964), for a popular account.

Additional material must be ferreted from biographies such as TEMPLE GAIRDNER OF CAIRO (London: S.P.C.K., 1930), by Constance Padwick; Archibald M. Hay, CHARLES INWOOD, HIS MINISTRY AND ITS SECRET (London: Marshall, 1929), and W. R. Wheeler, A MAN SENT FROM GOD: A BIOGRAPHY OF ROBERT E. SPEER[25] (Westwood, N.J.: Revell, 1956).

144

---

25. Robert Elliott Speer, a member of the Student Volunteer movement (See Neill, ed., CONCISE DICTIONARY OF THE CHRISTIAN WORLD MISSION [Nashville: Abingdon, 1971], pp. 571-572), and later senior secretary of the Board of Foreign Missions of the Presbyterian Church in the U.S.A., was a popular speaker at Keswick and at Moody's Northfield, Winona Lake, Indiana, and other "Keswick" conventions. A prolific author, he contributed to WINONA ECHOES, NORTHFIELD ECHOES and

The Missionary concerns are reflected today
by the many mission groups who recruit and
advertise at the Convention, by records of
missionary meetings published in the annual,
THE KESWICK WEEK, and by the multitude of
mission oriented articles appearing in the
weekly LIFE OF FAITH.

Conventions Abroad. LIFE OF FAITH continuously reports on "Keswick" conventions
throughout the world. John Pollock, THE KES-
WICK STORY (London: Hodder & Stoughton,
1964), p. 97, note 3, gives a list of several
"offshoots" with date of origin but is not
complete. SCOTLAND'S KESWICK: SKETCHES AND
REMINISCENCES (London: Marshall Bros., 1917),
by Norman C. Macfarlane chronicles the Convention there. THE MID-AMERICA KESWICK WEEK,
VITAL MESSAGES BY NINE CONTEMPORARY CHRISTIAN
LEADERS (Westwood, N.J.: Revell, 1960), is
the only published record of the meetings
held at Moody Memorial Church, Chicago since
1954. No registry of "Keswick" camps or conventions has been found.

THE FUNDAMENTALS (Vol. 3, 61-75; 12, 64-84).
His books focused on missions, ecclesiastical
unity and the internal life. See especially
the often reprinted, THE MARKS OF A MAN; OR,
THE ESSENTIALS OF CHRISTIAN CHARACTER (Cincinnati: Jennings & Graham, 1907); JESUS AND
OUR HUMAN PROBLEMS (N.Y.: Revell, 1946),
dealing with the relationship between Christ
and sin; THE MEANING OF CHRIST TO ME (N.Y.:
Revell, 1936), an exposition based on the
life of Christ; and THE FINALITY OF JESUS
CHRIST (N.Y.: Revell, 1933), given originally as the L.P. Stone Lectures at Princeton
Theological Seminary, 1932-1933 and The Gay
Lectures at the Southern Baptist Theological
Seminary, 1932-1933. See also K. S. Latour-
ette, "Speer, Robert E." in Neill, CONCISE
DICTIONARY OF THE CHRISTIAN WORLD MISSION,
pp. 565-566.

The Keswick Movement began almost immediately
to influence the American religious scene.
Keswick had received its impetus from American revivalism via the Robert Pearsall Smiths,
W. E. Boardman, Asa Mahan, Amanda Smith and
A. T. Pierson. These men and women were of
the perfectionist persuasion and leaned more
toward Arminian than toward Calvinistic theological categories regarding Christian spirituality. They were oriented toward thinking
in "crisis" language. Literature and folk-
lore are the recorders of the excesses en-
gendered.

The British leaders, mainly Anglican, had a
moderating influence on religious crisis enthusiasm (see below, Theological Distinctives).
Moody,[26] who had been perceived as a co-

146

26. Dwight Lyman Moody was the subject of
    biographies by two of his sons. William
R. Moody, THE LIFE OF DWIGHT L. MOODY (N.Y.:
Revell, 1900), provided "The Official Authorized Version," complete with tributes by F. B.
Meyer and G. Campbell Morgan. Paul D. Moody,
MY FATHER; AN INTIMATE PORTRAIT OF DWIGHT
MOODY (Boston: Little, Brown, 1938), gives
a picture of Moody as the warm, lovable, vi-
tal human being, which balances the rather
stiff quaint man portrayed in his THE SHORTER
LIFE OF D. L. MOODY (Chicago: Bible Insti-
tute Colportage Association, 1900). Accounts
of Moody's work in Europe may be found in the
ponderous dusty chronicles of John Hall, THE
AMERICAN EVANGELISTS, D. L. MOODY AND IRA D.
SANKEY, IN GREAT BRITAIN AND IRELAND (N.Y.:
Dodd & Mead, 1875), as well as in Edgar Johnson Goodspeed, A FULL HISTORY OF THE WONDER-
FUL CAREER OF MOODY AND SANKEY, IN GREAT BRIT-
AIN AND AMERICA ...(N.Y.: Henry S. Goodspeed,
1876).

More recently, J. C. Pollock, MOODY: A BIO-
GRAPHICAL PORTRAIT OF THE PACESETTER IN MOD-

laborer in revival by Smith, was quick to
transport the restrained spiritual expression
of Keswick back to his famed Northfield Conferences and to what became Moody Bible
Institute in Chicago.[27] (Go to next page)

ERN MASS EVANGELISM (N.Y.: Macmillan, 1963),
the British edition entitled, MOODY WITHOUT
SANKEY; A NEW BIOGRAPHICAL PORTRAIT (London:
Hodder & Stoughton, 1963), has rewritten
the story of Moody's life, but the lack of
documentation makes it of little value for
research.

James F. Findlay's Ph.D. thesis at the University of Chicago, published as DWIGHT L. MOODY,
AMERICAN EVANGELIST, 1837-1899 (Chicago:
University of Chicago, 1969), is by far the
best work available on Moody. Also indispensable is Wilbur M. Smith, AN ANNOTATED BIBLI-
OGRAPHY OF D.L. MOODY (Chicago: Moody, 1948).
With the inevitable omissions that plague
such an effort, it is carefully done, including previously unpublished materials.

Of particular interest for the discussion of
Holiness Movement-Keswick relations is the
"sanctification" experience of D. L. Moody
alluded to in his own writings and discussed
by Sarah A. Cooke, a Free Methodist layperson,
in THE HANDMAIDEN OF THE LORD; OR, WAYSIDE
SKETCHES (Chicago: Arnold, 1896), revised
and enlarged as WAYSIDE SKETCHES; OR, THE
HANDMAIDEN OF THE LORD (Grand Rapids: Shaw,
n.d.). Moody's experience was also discussed
several times by Asa Mahan in DIVINE LIFE.

27. Moody Bible Institute of Chicago, found-
     ed circa 1886, has been thoroughly stud-
ied by Gene A. Getz, MBI; THE STORY OF MOODY
BIBLE INSTITUTE (Chicago: Moody, 1969). A
careful effort is made to chronicle the outreach as well as the history of the institu-

R. A. Torrey,[28] Moody's choice for Director
of Chicago Bible Institute, spoke at Keswick;
Moody invited A.T. Pierson, H.W. Webb-Peploe,[29]

---

tion. The extensive bibliography, pp. 356-
369, must serve as a beginning for any additional research.

28.   Reuben Archer Torrey had a varied career
       as evangelist, author, and Bible School
leader. Apparently no extensive critical bio-
graphical examination of Torrey's contribu-
tion has been made. John Kennedy Maclean pub-
lished three small volumes: TORREY AND ALEX-
ANDER, THE STORY OF THEIR LIVES (London:
Partridge, 1905), TRIUMPHANT EVANGELISM: THE
THREE YEARS' MISSIONS OF DR. TORREY AND MR.
ALEXANDER IN GREAT BRITAIN AND IRELAND (Lon-
don: Marshall Bros., 1905), and UNDER TWO
MASTERS: THE STORY OF JACOBY, DR. TORREY'S
ASSISTANT (London: Marshall Bros., 1905).
All are popular and devotional but not very
helpful for understanding the man himself.
Torrey was particularly influential in com-
bining the concern for personal holiness with
millenarian concerns. THE BAPTISM WITH THE
HOLY SPIRIT (N.Y.: Revell, 1895), and THE
FUNDAMENTAL DOCTRINES OF THE CHRISTIAN FAITH
(N.Y.: Doran, 1918), were his most important
books. An able tractarian, he focused more
and more on eschatology; e.g., THE RETURN OF
THE LORD JESUS; THE KEY TO THE SCRIPTURE, AND
THE SOLUTION OF ALL OUR POLITICAL AND SOCIAL
PROBLEMS; OR, THE GOLDEN AGE THAT IS SOON
COMING TO THE EARTH (Los Angeles: Bible In-
stitute of L.A., 1913). Several of Torrey's
sermons and the tract, "Why God Used D. L.
Moody," were often printed in holiness jour-
nals.

29.   H. W. Webb-Peploe was a popular preacher
       at Keswick and Northfield. No major bi-
ography has been written. Barabas, SO GREAT

F. B. Meyer,[30] Andrew Murray,[31] and G. Camp-

_____

SALVATION, pp. 165-169, is the most extensive
"vita." Most of his writings are from various convention addresses. Most influential
were his sermons, THE VICTORIOUS LIFE, and
THE LIFE OF PRIVILEGE: POSSESSION, PEACE,
AND POWER (London: Nisbet, 1896, 1897). For
additional bibliography see Jones, A GUIDE TO
THE STUDY OF THE HOLINESS MOVEMENT.

30.   F. B. Meyer, "the best known Baptist
     clergyman of his day" (Barabas, SO GREAT
SALVATION, p. 182), was a vigorous proponent
of the Keswick message. Barabas (ibid., p.
186) observes, "It is doubtful whether any
other Keswick leader ever did more than Dr.
Meyer to make the distinctive Keswick message
known throughout the world." His life story
by W. Y. Fullerton, F. B. MEYER: A BIOGRAPHY
(London: Marshall, Morgan & Scott, 1929), is
a perceptive, highly readable account. M.
Jennie Street, F. B. MEYER: HIS LIFE AND
WORK (London: S. W. Partridge, 1902), is a
more popular account. See also Barabas, SO
GREAT SALVATION, pp. 182-186. The story of
his ministry at Leicester is found in F. B.
Meyer, THE BELLS OF IS; OR, VOICES OF HUMAN
NEED AND SORROW (London: Morgan & Scott,
1894). Here more than anywhere, the genius
of Meyer is revealed. An extensive listing
of his writings may be found in the advertise-
ments at the back of the book! A more traditional list, however, with incomplete bibliographic information and short title may be
found in chapter 24 of Fullerton.

31.   Andrew Murray, who spoke at "Keswick"
     meetings in America and England, spoke
most enduringly from his parish in South Africa through the pages of the SOUTH AFRICAN PI-
ONEER (see p. 82) and his often reprinted numerous books, pamphlets, and tracts. Of spe-

bell Morgan[32] to speak at Northfield. All
were prominent Keswick speakers. When in
1892 Moody was on an overseas crusade, A. J.
Gordon, Keswick speaker and Boston pastor,

---

cial significance are: THE SPIRIT OF CHRIST:
THOUGHTS ON THE INDWELLING OF THE HOLY SPIRIT
IN THE BELIEVER AND THE CHURCH (London: Nis-
bet, 1888; the American ed. of circa 1904 has
a biographical statement reprinted from the
SOUTH AFRICAN PIONEER); BACK TO PENTECOST:
THE FULFILLMENT OF "THE PROMISE OF THE FA-
THER" (ACTS 1:4) (London: Oliphants, 1918);
and HOLY IN CHRIST: THOUGHTS ON THE CALLING
OF GOD'S CHILDREN TO BE HOLY AS HE IS HOLY,
and THE TWO COVENANTS AND THE SECOND BLESSING
(London: Nisbet, 1888, 1889), in which are
set forth his concept of sanctification.
W. M. Douglas has summarized Murray's teaching in ANDREW MURRAY AND HIS MESSAGE: ONE OF
GOD'S CHOICE SAINTS (London: Oliphants,
1926); reprinted with some deletions, Fort
Washington, Pa.: Christian Literature Crusade, 1957. J. DuPlessis, THE LIFE OF ANDREW
MURRAY OF SOUTH AFRICA (London: Marshall
Bros., 1919), is a comparatively well written
biography. A valuable bibliography, unfortunately abbreviated, forms Appendix B, pp. 526
-535. The index is helpfully complete.

32. G. Campbell Morgan as a young man was
     rejected for ordination by the Wesleyan
Methodists. He became a popular and fre-
quent speaker both at Keswick and at Moody's
Northfield Conferences. John Harries,
G. CAMPBELL MORGAN, THE MAN AND HIS MINISTRY
(1930), is the best biography. Another, by
his daughter-in-law, Jill Morgan, is based on
his personal papers: A MAN OF THE WORD:
LIFE OF G. CAMPBELL MORGAN (1951). The
style, however, is awkward. THIS WAS HIS
FAITH: THE EXPOSITORY LETTERS OF G. CAMPBELL
MORGAN (1952), contains excerpts, topically

was left in charge of the meetings. Ernest
R. Sandeen,[33] THE ROOTS OF FUNDAMENTALISM:
BRITISH AND AMERICAN MILLENARIANISM, 1800-
1930 (Chicago: University of Chicago, 1970),
suggests that these meetings, and especially
F. B. Meyer, were influential in the adoption
of a Keswickian concern for a higher Christian life by the millenarians who were Calvinistic and conservative.

By 1913, an American Keswick Conference was
underway. Three volumes in particular are of
importance: VICTORY IN CHRIST: A REPORT OF
PRINCETON CONFERENCE 1916 (Philadelphia:
Board of Managers of Princeton Conf., 1916);
THE VICTORIOUS LIFE: MESSAGES FROM THE SUM-
MER CONFERENCES AT WHITTIER, CALIFORNIA, JUNE;
PRINCETON, NEW JERSEY, JULY; CEDAR LAKE, IN-
DIANA, AUGUST; INCLUDING ALSO SOME MESSAGES
FROM THE 1917 CONFERENCE AT PRINCETON AND
OTHER MATERIAL (Philadelphia: Board of Man-
agers of Victorious Life Conf., 1918), and THE
VICTORIOUS CHRIST: MESSAGES FROM CONFERENCES
HELD BY THE VICTORIOUS LIFE TESTIMONY IN 1922
(Philadelphia: Sunday School Times, 1923).
In the last volume is a brief historical

---

arranged. No data is included as to occa-
sion, recipient, etc. All the above were
published by Revell; each contains an incomplete list of his works. Harold Murray,
G. CAMPBELL MORGAN, BIBLE TEACHER: A SKETCH
OF THE GREAT EXPOSITOR AND EVANGELIST (London: Marshall, Morgan & Scott, 1938), is a
study on an important facet of Morgan's life.

33. Pp. 176-181, Sandeen, ROOTS OF FUNDAMEN-
TALISM is crucial for an understanding
of the deeper life movements within the U.S.
With careful precision he places the men and
issues in meaningful perspective. See especially Chapter 6, "The Prophecy and Bible
Conference Movement."

statement, "The Hour for America's Keswick" pps. 249-252, which ends in a plea for funds to support the new camp at Keswick, New Jersey.

The American Holiness Movement. While the Calvinistic branch of the deeper life movement was having considerable success in America, the Arminian branch was quickly losing its influence within Methodism and was being threatened by the successes of Pentecostalism, particularly in the South.[34] The sibling rivalry which developed has led to a hardening of both theological alternatives and to mutual caricature.

---

34.   See C. E. Jones, PERFECTIONIST PERSUASION: THE HOLINESS MOVEMENT IN AMERICAN METHODISM 1867-1936, A.T.L.A. Monograph Series,5 (Metuchen, N.J.: Scarecrow, 1975). This superb book, based upon the heretofore mentioned, "Perfectionist Persuasion: A Social Profile of the National Holiness Movement Within American Methodism, 1867-1936" (Ph.D. dissertation, University of Wisconsin, 1968), is available from University Microfilms, Ann Arbor, Mich., number 68-0, 083). He discusses the origins of Nazarene, Free Methodist, Wesleyan, et al; churches. Vinson Synan, THE HOLINESS-PENTECOSTAL MOVEMENT IN THE UNITED STATES (Grand Rapids: Eerdmans, 1971), traces Pentecostal incursions in the American Holiness Movement. Additional bibliographic material necessary to understand this period may be found in the first two volumes of "Occasional Bibliographic Papers of the B. L. Fisher Library": Donald W. Dayton, THE AMERICAN HOLINESS MOVEMENT: A BIBLIOGRAPHIC INTRODUCTION, now undergoing substantial revision, and David W. Faupel, THE AMERICAN PENTECOSTAL MOVEMENT: A BIBLIOGRAPHIC ESSAY (Wilmore, Kentucky, Asbury Theological Seminary, 1971-1972).

The Holiness-Keswick debate focused on two issues: original sin and the nature of sanctification. Holiness Movement clergy in the Methodist-Wesleyan context emphasized the instantaneous removal of original sin by an instantaneous act of grace; viz, entire sanctification. Keswick maintained a Reformed view of sin and a gradual process of sanctification. The categories became "eradicationist" (Keswick term for the Holiness position) versus "suppressionist" (Holiness Movement term for the Keswick position). Suppression described the Keswickian goal of "uniform sustained victory over known sin." There was agreement regarding the need for sanctification. The difference arose regarding its meaning for the believer. It has been suggested that Asa Mahan dropped out of the Keswick Convention after the first three; he reportedly observed at Brighton, "It doesn't go deep enough."

W. B. Godbey,[35] radical Holiness Movement preacher, teacher, and influential pamphleteer, was one of the first to rise to the attack. KESWICKISM (Louisville, Ky.: Pentecostal Publishing House, n.d.), discusses the absoluteness of the destruction of sin, then moves to an account of "My Keswickal Convention" in Madras, India. He comments on the lack of spiritual power on the part of those in attendance, observing:

...The truth of the matter is, their

---

35. On William B. Godbey see his AUTOBIOGRAPHY (Cincinnati: God's Revivalist Office, 1909), and his comments a year before his death, HAPPY NONAGENARIAN (Zarephath, N.J.: Pillar of Fire, 1919). For additional bibliography,though not complete, see Jones, A GUIDE TO THE STUDY OF THE HOLINESS MOVEMENT. A critical biography has not been published.

experience is simply a good case
of regeneration, as they only
claim to have sin suppressed and
kept down by grace in a subjugat-
ed state, so that it does not
break out and commit actual trans-
gression. (p. 48)...Keswickism is
a deficiency rather than a heresy
... (p. 59)...Keswickism as a nor-
mal consequence breaks down, because the Holy Ghost will not a-
bide, while old Adam remains in
the heart" (p. 61).

About 1910, A. M. Hills,[36] a Nazarene educa-
tor and writer, wrote SCRIPTURAL HOLINESS
AND KESWICK TEACHING COMPARED (Manchester:
Star Hall, n.d.), which for years has been
the standard Holiness Movement critique of
the Keswick Movement. Part I presents "Scriptural Holiness Teaching," arguing for a "second blessing" and "the eradication of car-
nality," and describing the reception and con-
tinuance in this "life of blessing" which is
"the longing of devout souls." Part II, "A
Review of Keswick Teaching," although undocumented, features quotations from Keswick
speakers as reported in KESWICK WEEK. He com-
mends Keswick teachers for attempting to lift
the moral tone of the era, but notes that
"Keswick teachers are not consistent with
themselves, nor in agreement with each other,"
that their teaching is "painfully indistinct,"
that "much of what these preachers call holi-

---

36. Aaron Merritt Hills (1848-1935) supplied
      a short autobiographical statement to
PENTECOSTAL MESSENGERS (Cincinnati: M. W.
Knapp, 1898), and the FULL SALVATION QUARTERLY,
Vol. 5 (1899?). See also H. O. Wiley, "Dr.
A. M. Hills," HERALD OF HOLINESS, Vol. 40
(July 2, 1951), p. 388, and James McGraw,
"The Preaching of A. M. Hills," PREACHER'S
MAGAZINE, Vol. 33, No. 2 (1958), p.6-8.

ness is only regeneration," and that they maintain an "unsound philosophy about self, and the nature of flesh and depravity." Hills' massive analysis lacks coherency, the logic is often circular, and he clearly does not understand the Keswick theological method and position. He furnishes a caricature rather than an exposé of Keswickian teaching.

H. A. Baldwin,[37] a Free Methodist[38] pastor and writer, published a curious little volume, OBJECTIONS TO ENTIRE SANCTIFICATION CONSIDERED (Pittsburgh: Published for the Author, 1911), containing short refutations to sixteen "Objections." "Keswickism" is described as "one of the most dangerous enemies of the experience of holiness...for they give us to understand that such a thing as the entire eradication of the carnal nature from the soul is an impossibility in this world" (p. 11). Quoting the famed Daniel Steele, Baldwin argues the Holiness Movement case on the radical nature of New Testament language regarding sanctification and the eradication of the carnal nature, but offers the ameliorating observation that only God knows the heart of man!

The Keswickian perspective was asserted by

---

37. Harmon Allen Baldwin, OBJECTIONS TO ENTIRE-SANCTIFICATION CONSIDERED has recently been reprinted by H. E. Schmul in HOLINESS CLASSICS, NO. I. (Titusville, Pa.: The Allegheny Wesleyan Methodist Connection, 1973). Refer to C. E. Jones for biographical and bibliographical data currently available.

38. For bibliographical direction on the Free Methodist Church, see Donald W. Dayton, THE AMERICAN HOLINESS MOVEMENT, A BIBLIOGRAPHIC INTRODUCTION and C. E. Jones, A GUIDE TO THE STUDY OF THE HOLINESS MOVEMENT.

the indefatigable H. A. Ironside[39] in the often reprinted HOLINESS, THE FALSE AND THE
TRUE (New York: Loizeaux Brothers, 1912).
He chronicles, in fiercely polemical fashion,
his early frustrations as a member of the Salvation Army,[40] and attacks the level of spirituality within the Holiness Movement as a
unit. Moving from the autobiographical to
the doctrinal, Ironside argues for a progressive view of sanctification whereby the Christian comes to live victoriously over tempta-
tion and doubt: "All efforts to attain sinless perfection in this world can only end in
failure," (p. 132). "Only as one learns to
refuse everything that is of the flesh, and
finds everything in Christ, will...be enjoyed
a life lived in fellowship with God" (p. 133).

Henry E. Brockett, SCRIPTURAL FREEDOM FROM
SIN: A DEFENSE OF THE PRECIOUS TRUTH OF EN-
TIRE SANCTIFICATION BY FAITH AND AN EXAMINA-
TION OF THE DOCTRINE OF "THE TWO NATURES"
(Kansas City, Mo.: Nazarene, 1941), is pri-
marily a critique of Ironside's polemic. Re-
stating the classical American perfectionist
doctrine of entire sanctification, he relies
heavily upon A. M. Hills, SCRIPTURAL HOLI-
NESS AND KESWICK TEACHING COMPARED.

The controversy continued, often implicitly,
in the pulpits and periodicals of both per-

---

39. H. A. Ironside was a powerful American
    expositor and teacher. Closely identi-
fied with the American deeper life movement,
he was a frequent "Bible Camp" speaker and
for nineteen years, 1930-1948, was pastor of
Moody Memorial Church (THE MOODY CHURCH STORY,
n.d., n.p., 20 pps.), Chicago, the "campus"
church of Moody Bible Institute.

40. For bibliographical direction on The Sal-
    vation Army, see below under "Bibliogra-
phy." Dayton and Jones are particularly helpful.

spectives, although little of a scholarly nature was published until the 1960's, when the Holiness Movement began to wrestle with its identity, theologically and historically. Papers prepared originally for a National Holiness Association study group included George E. Failing, "Developments in Holiness Theology after Wesley" and Everett L. Cattell, "An Appraisal of the Keswick and Wesleyan Contemporary Positions," published as INSIGHTS INTO HOLINESS, compiled by Kenneth Geiger (Kansas City, Mo.: Beacon Hill, 1962). Both papers constitute cautious attempts to understand the relationship between Keswick and Holiness alternatives. Another of these papers was presented by W. Ralph Thompson to the Wesleyan Theological Society as "An Appraisal of the Keswick and Wesleyan Contemporary Positions," WESLEYAN THEOLOGICAL JOURNAL Vol. 1 (1966), p. 11-20. Thompson is more polemic but encourages the two sides to learn from each other:

> "Keswickism is weak in its scriptural foundation, but strong in its proclamation. Wesleyanism is doctrinally sound, but lacks in zeal and in positive presentation" (pp. 19-20).

More recently, Melvin E. Dieter, a Wesleyan,[41] has investigated the origins of the Keswick Movement, the early years of the subsequent revival and efforts at institutionalization within the various expressions of "Revivalism." Dieter presents by far the most balanced scholarly analysis from within the Holiness Movement.

The American Pentecostal Movement. Both W. B.

---

41. For material relevant to The Wesleyan Church, see below: "Bibliography." Dayton and Dieter are especially helpful.

Godbey and A. M. Hills, who polemicized contra a Keswickian position, also lifted their
pens to refute Pentecostalism.[42]   David W.
Faupel, THE AMERICAN PENTECOSTAL MOVEMENT, A
BIBLIOGRAPHICAL ESSAY ("Occasional Bibliographic Papers of the B. L. Fisher Library," 2.
Wilmore, Ky.: Asbury Theological Seminary,
1972), originally published in the 1972 SUM-
MARY OF PROCEEDINGS: AMERICAN THEOLOGICAL
LIBRARY ASSOCIATION, lists fourteen Pentecostal denominations that do not subscribe to a
Wesleyan understanding of sanctification, but
adopt a Keswickian position. William Menzies
of Evangel College, Springfield, Missouri, in
1973 presented to the Society for Pentecostal
Studies, Cleveland, Tennessee, a paper entitled, "The Non-Wesleyan Origins of the Pentecostal Movement" (photocopy, 10 pps.). He
asserts that Alexander Dowie, A. B. Simpson,
founder of the Christian and Missionary Alliance and A. J. Gordon were influential in
the promotion of Keswick doctrines. He details (pages 5-9) the subsequent controversy
between Wesleyan and Keswickian types of holiness doctrine within Pentecostal groups.
Melvin Dieter read a paper before the Society
for Pentecostal Studies, Cleveland, Tennessee,
1973, "Wesleyan-Holiness Aspects of Pentecostal Origins: As Mediated through the Nineteenth Century Holiness Revivals" (30 pps.
photocopy), in which he traces the influence
of the Holiness Movement which, as noted a-
bove, also provided stimulus for the Keswick
Convention. Menzies' and Dieter's papers

158

---

42. W. B. Godbey, SPIRITUAL GIFTS AND GRACES
     (Cincinnati: God's Revivalist Office,
1895), defines tongues as languages and encourages all to seek this "gift." Later, he
wrote the acidic TONGUE MOVEMENT, SATANIC
(Zarephath, N.J.: Pillar of Fire, 1918). A.
M. Hills wrote THE TONGUES MOVEMENT (Manchester, Eng.: Star Hall, 1910), to refute the
claims of the burgeoning Pentecostalism.

will soon be more readily available in a volume by Logos Press containing papers presented to the Society for Pentecostal Studies in 1972. The papers focus around the theme, "Aspects of Pentecostal Origins."

The Christian and Missionary Alliance. Note: Publications mentioned in the following paragraphs, except where otherwise indicated, were published by the Christian Alliance, New York, and currently by its successor, Christian Publications, Harrisburg, Pa. In 1974 the International Headquarters of the C. & M. A. was moved from New York City to Upper Nyack, New York. The Christian and Missionary Alliance originated in the 1880's under the direction of A. B. Simpson, pastor of 13th Street Presbyterian Church in New York City.[43] Frustrated in ministry and plagued by illness, he was influenced by the faith healing and millenarian hopes of A. J. Gordon,[44] THE MIN-

43. From 1887-1897 the Christian Alliance was Simpson's domestic association, and The International Missionary Alliance was devoted to foreign missions. The "merger" produced the C. & M. A.

44. Adoniram Judson Gordon (1836-1895) was an influential Baptist in America and a leader of the millenarian movement (Sandeen, THE ROOTS OF FUNDAMENTALISM, passim). He exercised much influence in the early synthesis of the C. & M. A., primarily through the book mentioned above and through his often reprinted THE MINISTRY OF THE SPIRIT, with an introduction by F. B. Meyer (Philadelphia: American Baptist Pub. Soc., 1894). Also important is THE TWOFOLD LIFE: OR, CHRIST'S WORK FOR US, AND CHRIST'S WORK IN US (Boston: H. Gannett, 1883), a study in the attainment of "the abundant life." His autobiography is HOW CHIRST CAME TO CHURCH; THE PASTOR'S DREAM: A SPIRIT-

ISTRY OF HEALING: OR, MIRACLES OF CURE IN ALL
AGES (Boston: H. Gannett, 1882), and W. E.
Boardman (see above, note 13). Concerned for
evangelism among the underprivileged both at
home and abroad, Simpson withdrew from the
Presbyterian Church, founding the new Alli-
ance around the fourfold doctrine of Christ
as Saviour, Sanctifier, Healer, and Coming
King. Simpson's writings emphasize these con-
cerns: THE FOUR-FOLD GOSPEL (1925), THE FUL-
NESS OF JESUS; OR CHRISTIAN LIFE IN THE NEW
TESTAMENT (1890), LIFE MORE ABUNDANTLY (1912),
WALKING IN THE SPIRIT (n.d.), WHOLLY SANCTI-
FIED (1925), THE GOSPEL OF HEALING (1915),
(all of the above are being made available in
paperback), THE LORD FOR THE BODY, WITH QUES-
TIONS AND ANSWERS ON DIVINE HEALING (1925),
an enlargement of the earlier THE DISCOVERY
OF DIVINE HEALING (1903), THE COMING ONE
(1912) and HEAVEN OPENED: OR, EXPOSITIONS OF
THE BOOK OF REVELATION (1899).

160

Simpson's life, chronicled by A. E. Thompson,
THE LIFE OF A. B. SIMPSON: WITH SPECIAL CHAP-
TERS BY PAUL RADER, JAMES M. GRAY, J. GREGORY
MANTLE, R. H. GLOVER, KENNETH MACKENZIE, F. H.
SENFT, AND W. M. TURNBULL (1920), was revised
as A. B. SIMPSON: HIS LIFE AND WORK (1939).
A. W. Tozer, WINGSPREAD: ALBERT B. SIMPSON,
A STUDY IN SPIRITUAL ALTITUDE (Centenary ed.,
1943), is an exposition of his life.

Studies of the historical development of the
Christian and Missionary Alliance are George
P. Pardington, TWENTY-FIVE WONDERFUL YEARS,
1889-1914: A POPULAR SKETCH OF THE CHRISTIAN

UAL AUTOBIOGRAPHY, BY A. J. GORDON...WITH THE
LIFE-STORY, AND THE DREAM AS INTERPRETING THE
MAN, BY A. T. PIERSON (Philadelphia: Amer.
Baptist Pub. Soc., 1895). His son, Ernest B.
Gordon, wrote ADONIRAM JUDSON GORDON, A BIOG-
RAPHY (New York: Revell, 1896).

AND MISSIONARY ALLIANCE (1914), and AFTER FIF-
TY YEARS: A RECORD OF GOD'S WORKING THROUGH
THE CHRISTIAN AND MISSIONARY ALLIANCE, by R.
B. Ekvall et al. (1939). Samuel J. Stoesz,
UNDERSTANDING MY CHURCH (1968), is intended
as a manual for church members and is a good
survey of history, doctrine and polity, unfor-
tunately without bibliography. J. H. Hunter's
75th anniversary volume was devoted to a
study of mission work, BESIDE ALL WATERS; THE
STORY OF SEVENTY-FIVE YEARS OF WORLD-WIDE MIN-
ISTRY: THE CHRISTIAN AND MISSIONARY ALLIANCE
(1964). Mission work is also chronicled in
MISSIONARY ATLAS: A MANUAL OF THE FOREIGN
WORK OF THE CHRISTIAN AND MISSIONARY ALLIANCE,
(4th ed., 1964; 1st ed. 1936).

The Christian and Missionary Alliance has produced significant missionary policy material;
for example, Louis L. King, "A Presentation
of the Indigenous Church Policy of the Christian and Missionary Alliance" (photocopy 17
pps., 1961?). They sponsored and published
the REPORT OF PROCEEDINGS of the Afro-Asia
Alliance Literature Conference, April, 1963
(1964),hoping to strengthen indigenous work.
A rich heritage of missionary biography includes Russell T. Hitt, CANNIBAL VALLEY (1962),
a story of Dutch New Guinea, and James C. Hef-
ley, BY LIFE OR BY DEATH (Grand Rapids: Zondervan, 1969), about missionary efforts in
Indo-China.

The most influential theologian of the Christian and Missionary Alliance has been George
P. Pardington, THE CRISIS OF THE DEEPER LIFE[45]
(1906), who defined the Keswick orientation
toward sanctification to be adopted by the denomination. With his conciliatory language,

---

45. Pardington, THE CRISIS OF THE DEEPER
    LIFE, along with several volumes by A. W.
Tozer have been reprinted in paperback by
Christian Pub., Harrisburg, Pa.

the Christian and Missionary Alliance has
been able to maintain close relationship with
the American Holiness Movement, although it
has remained outside the orb of the National
Holiness Association. It is particularly im-
pressive that the Christian and Missionary
Alliance did not develop a hostile polemic
contra Pentecostalism as did the Holiness
Movement, but maintains an attitude of "seek
not, forbid not" to this day. A. W. Tozer,
Oswald J. Smith, and of course, A. B. Simpson
have been the important Christian and Missionary Alliance expositors. For additional bibliography see C. E. Jones, A GUIDE TO THE
STUDY OF THE HOLINESS MOVEMENT, which contains the most complete bibliography to date
on the Christian and Missionary Alliance.

LITERATURE OF KESWICK

The literature produced under the impetus of
the Keswick Movement falls into three over-
lapping categories: theological, biblical,
and devotional studies. With regard to this
extensive corpus of literature, several problems arise. First, the Keswick Convention
in England has never defined a precise theological perspective. Rather, "Keswick theology" tends to revolve around a few "guiding
lights" who, in each generation, have managed
to keep on a track consistent with the heritage of the movement. Throughout, the concern has been for "practical holiness," for
the experience of the power of God within the
life of the believer. There is no creedal
statement, merely a rather remarkable consen-
sus of theological orientation. It is very
different in America. The American "Keswick"
people bought quickly and deeply into the Mil-
lenarian-Fundamentalist strictness of doctrine, while attempting to maintain the British experiential emphasis. R. A. Torrey, A.
T. Pierson, H. A. Ironside and F. B. Meyer
were involved in producing THE FUNDAMENTALS
(Chicago: Testimony Publishing House, 1910-

1915). R. A. Torrey together with A. C. Dixon and Louis Meyer edited this influential
series which continues to express the creed
of American fundamentalism. Thus, the rep-
resentatives of American "Keswick" tend to be
more concerned with correct (conservative)
thinking than with the experiential aspects
of the Christian life. Both American and British Keswickians endeavor to be "based on the
Bible."

The method of this portion of the essay is to
divide the literature according to its emphases. Theological Studies will present literature which addresses a concern of doctrine,
focusing on the issue. Devotional Studies
will be considered the work of authors who,
in summary or synthetic fashion, devote themselves to explicating Christian spirituality.
Biblical Studies involve major expositions,
commentaries and Bible study aids.

Bibliography

The Keswick Convention has not produced institutions which in turn would carefully define
what is to be considered "Keswick" or not
"Keswick." Keswick has remained a Convention,
that is, a loosely associated group concerned
with the deeper life, and has generally been
ignored by church historians. Thus the state
of bibliographic research is sadly lacking.
The Keswick Movement is not treated in the
various standard bibliographic tools;however,
THE BRITISH MUSEUM GENERAL CATALOGUE OF PRINT-
ED BOOKS is somewhat helpful in finding works
of a personage associated with the movement.
The bibliographic sources which are available
have been cited in the preceding section.

Theological Studies

Keswickian concern for "practical holiness"
began with a heavy emphasis on Christian experience, an inheritance left by the crusad-

ing American evangelists. W. E. Boardman whose THE HIGHER CHRISTIAN LIFE, and IN THE POWER OF THE SPIRIT were influential in Keswick origins, stressed a second crisis experience. Asa Mahan, THE BAPTISM OF THE HOLY GHOST (New York: Palmer, 1870), and SCRIPTURE DOCTRINE OF CHRISTIAN PERFECTION (Boston: D. S. King, 1839), later published as CHRISTIAN PERFECTION (London: F. E. Longley,1875), emphasized the possibility of immediate attainment of Christian perfection, as did Robert Pearsall Smith, HOLINESS THROUGH FAITH, LIGHT ON THE WAY OF HOLINESS. Although he discounted sinless perfection, he retained the experiential and crisis-oriented language.

The resulting excess of religious enthusiasm was problematic for the early Keswick Convention as it sought acceptance for its participants and doctrines within the established church. The American heritage was played down and Keswickians began tracing their heritage to earlier authors(see above, note 4) and especially to Walter Marshall, THE GOSPEL-MYSTERY OF SANCTIFICATION, OPENED IN SUNDRY PRACTICAL DIRECTIONS: SUITED ESPECIALLY TO THE CASE OF THOSE WHO ARE UNDER THE GUILT AND POWER OF INDWELLING SIN, TO WHICH IS ADDED A SERMON ON JUSTIFICATION (Glasgow: Duncan and Robertson, 1797), original London edition 1692, edited and reprinted by Andrew Murray under the title, SANCTIFICATION, OR THE HIGHWAY OF HOLINESS (London: Nisbet, 1884). Marshall emphasized simplicity of faith and waiting on Christ as requirements for sanctification, and the resultant joy and peace of conscience. This book is devoid of the "religious enthusiasm" and "perfectionism" of the later American writers, and draws heavily upon the Scriptures in explicating sanctification in a winsome nonpolemic manner.

Other competent Keswick leaders developed and re-emphasized this approach to the issue. H. C. G. Moule, THOUGHTS ON CHRISTIAN SANCTI-

TY (London: Seeley, 1885), (reprinted by
Moody Press, Chicago, n.d.),consisting primarily of sermons delivered to the Cambridge
University Church Society, presents a careful
exposition of sanctification as self-surren-
der, and the personal power of "Jesus Christ
who lives for me and in me" (p. 93). Moule,[46]

46. Handley Carr Glyn Moule, Principal of
Ridley Hall, Cambridge and later successor of B. F. Westcott as Bishop of Durham had
a much needed stabilizing effect on Keswick.
His careful exegetical studies served to keep
the Convention from excesses which might have
destroyed its effectiveness. His biographers
were Keswick men. John Harford Battersby and
Frederick Charles Macdonald, HANDLEY CARR
GLYN MOULE, BISHOP OF DURHAM, A BIOGRAPHY
(London: Hodder & Stoughton, n.d. 1922?),is
a rather traditional biography based on his
letters and papers. John Baird, THE SPIRITUAL
UNFOLDING OF BISHOP H. C. G. MOULE, D.D., AN
EXPOSITION (London: Oliphants, n.d. 1926),is
of little value, being primarily an apology
for an evangelical perspective. See also the
briefer notes in OXFORD DICTIONARY OF THE
CHRISTIAN CHURCH, p. 930; DICTIONARY OF NA-
TIONAL BIOGRAPHY 1912-1921, p. 390-391 and
Barabas, SO GREAT SALVATION, 169-175. A com-
plete list of his works can be found in Bat-
tersby and Macdonald. Of primary interest
are JUSTIFYING RIGHTEOUSNESS (London: Seeley,
1885), OUTLINES OF CHRISTIAN DOCTRINE (London:
Hodder & Stoughton, 1889), VENI CREATOR
(London: Hodder & Stoughton, 1890), PHILIP-
PIAN STUDIES (London: Hodder & Stoughton,
1897), COLOSSIAN STUDIES (London: Hodder &
Stoughton, 1898), EPHESIAN STUDIES (London:
Hodder & Stoughton, 1900). NEED AND FULNESS
(London: Marshall Bros., 1895),is a series
of six addresses included in the KESWICK LI-
BRARY. PATIENCE AND COMFORT (1896) and
CHRIST AND THE CHRISTIAN (1919) are addresses

through his books, as well as his frequent appearances at the Keswick Convention, wielded a crucial, formative influence on the theological outlook of the Convention.

Alexander Smellie,[47] LIFT UP YOUR HEARTS: FOUR ADDRESSES ON SANCTIFICATION (London: Andrew Melrose,1915), a volume dedicated to Evan Hopkins, promotes the concept of achieving holiness through quiet surrender of self, holiness which, "though it is perfect, it is being perfected," (p. 65). However, Hopkins, THE LAW OF LIBERTY IN THE SPIRITUAL LIFE (1884), is the first orderly and extensive analysis of the essentials of the Christian life from a Keswickian perspective.

The Keswickian view of sin, first expounded in print by Hopkins, has been given additional exposition in H. C. G. Moule, NEED AND FULNESS (London: Marshall Bros., 1894), and OUTLINES OF CHRISTIAN DOCTRINE (London: Hodder & Stoughton, 1889), which, together with W. H. Griffith Thomas,[48] THE PRINCIPLES OF THEOLO-

---

delivered at Keswick on the subject of the Christian life and subsequently published by Marshall Brothers.

47. Alexander Smellie, the biographer of Evan Henry Hopkins, was a prolific producer of devotional material. GIVE ME THE MASTER (London: Andrew Melrose, 1906), IN THE HOUR OF SILENCE, A BOOK OF DAILY MEDITATIONS FOR A YEAR (London: Andrew Melrose, 1899), LIFT UP YOUR HEARTS, FOUR ADDRESSES ON SANCTIFICATION (London: Andrew Melrose, 1915),and WAYFARERS' DAILY MESSAGE (London: Marshall, Morgan & Scott, 1933-), are among his best productions. See Pollock, THE KESWICK CONVENTION, passim, for additional details.

48. William Henry Griffith Thomas has not yet been the subject of a biographer.

GY: AN INTRODUCTION TO THE THIRTY-NINE AR-
TICLES (London: Longmans, Green, 1930), and
R. W. Dale,[49] CHRISTIAN DOCTRINE (London:
Hodder & Stoughton, 1894), is about as close
to systematic theology as Keswickians have
attained. John Laidlaw, a professor of sys-
tematic theology at New College, Edinburgh,
worked with the problem of sin in THE BIBLE
DOCTRINE OF MAN: OR, THE ANTHROPOLOGY AND
PSYCHOLOGY OF SCRIPTURE (Edinburgh: Clark,
1879), and FOUNDATION TRUTHS OF SCRIPTURE AS
TO SIN AND SALVATION (Edinburgh: Clark,
1897). More popular in presentation are A.
T. Pierson, SHALL WE CONTINUE IN SIN? A VI-
TAL QUESTION FOR BELIEVERS ANSWERED IN THE
WORD OF GOD (London: Marshall Bros., 1897),
and Jessie Penn-Lewis, THE WARFARE WITH SATAN
AND THE WAY OF VICTORY (Leicester: "Over-
comer" Book Room, 1906), often reprinted.
Steven Barabas, SO GREAT SALVATION, and THE
KESWICK WEEK, unfortunately not indexed, con-
tain discussions of the nature of sin. Sev-
eral addresses from the latter were selected
and edited by Herbert F. Stevenson in KES-
WICK'S TRIUMPHANT VOICE: FORTY-EIGHT OUT-
STANDING ADDRESSES DELIVERED AT THE KESWICK
CONVENTION, 1882-1962 (London: Marshall, Mor-
gan & Scott, 1963), and KESWICK'S AUTHENTIC
VOICE: SIXTY-FIVE DYNAMIC ADDRESSES DELIVER-
ED AT THE KESWICK CONVENTION, 1875-1957 (Lon-
don: Marshall, Morgan & Scott, 1959). The
view of sin held unofficially by Keswick is
Reformed and Anglican, rather than the Wes-
leyan understanding of Mahan, Boardman, and
Arthur.

Some data is available in THE NEW INTERNATION-
AL DICTIONARY OF THE CHRISTIAN CHURCH, ed. J.
D. Douglas (Grand Rapids: Zondervan, 1974).
An ardent Anglican, he sought to serve his
church as a teacher and scholar.

49. A. W. W. Dale, THE LIFE OF R. W. DALE OF
     BIRMINGHAM (London: Hodder & Stoughton,

Quite understandably, the primary focus of
theological effort has been related to an understanding of the Holy Spirit and the Holy
Spirit's work in the believer's life; that
is, personal holiness. As mentioned above,
Moule, Smellie and Hopkins led the way in the
formulation of a Keswickian view of sanctification. Hopkins, THE LAW OF LIBERTY IN THE
SPIRITUAL LIFE views "Sanctification. ...as a
process; that is, as a work wrought in the
soul of the believer by the Holy Spirit, subsequently to regeneration." (p. 62) He quotes
"Owen on the Work of the Holy Spirit: 'It is
begun at once, and carried on gradually.'"
He sees sanctification as "a progressive and
gradual development of the new creation within the believer" (p. 63).

William MacDowall Aitken, THE HIGHWAY OF HOLI-
NESS: HELPS TO THE SPIRITUAL LIFE (London:
Shaw, 1883), picks up Hopkins' emphasis, warn-
ing against both spiritual dejection about
one's "state of grace" and antinomianism.
James Elder Cumming, "THROUGH THE ETERNAL
SPIRIT": A BIBLE STUDY ON THE HOLY GHOST
(Stirling: Drummond's Tract Depot, 1891),
is a lucid, more sophisticated treatment of
the nature and work of the Holy Spirit. H.
C. G. Moule contributed to the discussion,
VENI CREATOR: THOUGHTS ON THE PERSON AND
WORK OF THE HOLY SPIRIT OF PROMISE (London:
Hodder & Stoughton, 1890), an exposition on
personal holiness, and an anthology of ser-
mons, CHRIST IS ALL: SERMONS FROM NEW TESTA-
MENT TEXTS ON VARIOUS ASPECTS OF THE GLORY
AND WORK OF CHRIST (London: Sampson, Low,
1892), reprinted in the EXPOSITOR'S LIBRARY
(London: Hodder & Stoughton, 1912). Both

1898) is the biography by a son of this so-
cially concerned Congregationalist pastor-
theologian. See also OXFORD DICTIONARY OF
THE CHRISTIAN CHURCH, p. 369.

volumes represent a concern that the quest
for Christian holiness occur within Christo-
centric perceptions of the workings of God.

Written at the suggestion of, and dedicated
to the memory of George H. C. MacGregor,[50]
THE THINGS OF THE SPIRIT: TEACHING OF THE
WORD OF GOD ABOUT THE SPIRIT OF GOD (London:
Marshall Bros., 1898),is a Bible survey by G.
Campbell Morgan. Morgan, THE SPIRIT OF GOD
(New York: Revell, 1900), is an effort to re-
interpret a Keswickian understanding of the
Holy Spirit in light of the burgeoning dis-
pensationalist model of the spiritual his-
tory of the world. The latter work found pop-
ularity primarily in America.

Andrew Murray, the prolific South African author, who was introduced to the higher life
by Bishop William Taylor of the Methodist
Episcopal Church and a member of the National
Holiness Association,has influenced greatly
the development of spirituality within the
deeper life movement of Europe and America by
his often reprinted writings: ABSOLUTE SUR-
RENDER AND OTHER ADDRESSES (New York: Revell,
1897); THE FULL BLESSING OF PENTECOST: THE
ONE THING NEEDFUL (New York: Revell, 1908),
a manual on being "filled with the Spirit of
God"; THE SPIRIT OF CHRIST: THOUGHTS ON THE
INDWELLING OF THE HOLY SPIRIT IN THE BELIEVER
AND THE CHURCH (London: Nisbet, 1888); BE
PERFECT! A MESSAGE FROM THE FATHER IN HEAVEN
TO HIS CHILDREN ON EARTH (Chicago: Revell,
1894), in Revell's THE BLESSED LIFE SERIES
featuring works of F. B. Meyer and Andrew Mur-
ray; "LOVE MADE PERFECT" (London: Marshall
Bros., 1894); and THE NEW LIFE (London: Nis-

---

50. The life-story is narrated by his son,
    Duncan Campbell MacGregor, GEORGE H. C.
MACGREGOR, M. A., A BIOGRAPHY (London: Hodder & Stoughton, 1900).

bet, 1891), revised and abridged by Bethany
Fellowship, Minneapolis, 1965, presenting
"the holy life of obedience and of fruitful-
ness in which the Holy Spirit teaches us to
walk" (p. 12).

F. B. Meyer, THE WAY INTO THE HOLIEST, EXPOSI-
TIONS OF THE EPISTLE TO THE HEBREWS (London:
Morgan & Scott, 1893), presents in sermons a
chronicle of the Christian progression toward holiness. THE CHRIST-LIFE FOR THE SELF-
LIFE, also published as A CASTAWAY (Chicago:
Bible Institute Colportage Association, 1897),
is a more conventional anthology on the holy
life.

During the somewhat troubled period following
the change of leadership from the "old-guard"
of Hopkins, Webb-Peploe and Moule to John
Harford,[51] son of John Harford Battersby, and
to J. Stuart Holden, literary production tap-
ered off as did the success of the Conventions in the tempestuous war era. From this
period of transition come J. Stuart Holden,
REDEEMING VISION, a study of the possibilities of holy living, and THE PRICE OF POWER,
both published by Revell, 1908. W. H. Griffith Thomas, the remarkable scholar of the
holy life, contributed three important volumes. The most comprehensive, THE PRINCIPLES
OF THEOLOGY, AN INTRODUCTION TO THE THIRTY-
NINE ARTICLES (London: Longmans, Green, 1930),
published posthumously, presents a traditional Anglican-Keswickian conceptualization of
theology. Of excellent workmanship, it remains a valuable resource. THE HOLY SPIRIT
OF GOD (London: Longmans, 1913), is a thorough,

---

51. Canon John Harford added Battersby to
his Harford surname. Battersby was
dropped by most of his descendants. See C.
F. Harford, KESWICK CONVENTION (London: Marshall Bros., 1907), p. 51.

biblical, historical and systematic study of
the person and work of the Holy Spirit, originally given in 1913 as the L. P. Stone Lectures at Princeton Theological Seminary. Appended is a series of "Notes" on topics such
as tongues, laying on of hands, the baptism
of the Spirit, etc., and a bibliography, with
the overwhelming majority of titles referring
to Keswickian sources. Also see his THE ES-
SENTIALS OF LIFE (London: Pickering & Inglis,
1935), GRACE AND POWER: SOME ASPECTS OF THE
SPIRITUAL LIFE (New York: Revell, 1916), and
CHRISTIANITY IS CHRIST (London: Nisbet,
1909).

Of import far in excess of its modest size, W.
Graham Scroggie, THE FULNESS OF THE HOLY SPIR-
IT (Chicago: Bible Colportage Assn., 1925,
22 pps.),is an address given at the Moody Bi-
ble Institute of Chicago and published orig-
inally in the May 1925 issue of THE MOODY
MONTHLY. It is a concise summary of a Kes-
wickian understanding of sanctification.
Less concise, but of continuing influence in
Keswick circles is John Charles Ryle, HOLI-
NESS: ITS NATURE, HINDRANCES, DIFFICULTIES,
AND ROOTS (London: Hunt, 1879), reprinted
with an introduction by D. Martyn Lloyd-Jones
(London: Clarke, 1956).

Of momentous significance are three volumes
by J. Sidlow Baxter: A NEW CALL TO HOLINESS:
A RESTUDY AND RESTATEMENT OF NEW TESTAMENT
TEACHING CONCERNING CHRISTIAN SANCTIFICATION;
HIS DEEPER WORK IN US: A FURTHER INQUIRY IN-
TO NEW TESTAMENT TEACHING ON THE SUBJECT OF
CHRISTIAN HOLINESS; and OUR HIGH CALLING: A
SERIES OF DEVOTIONAL AND PRACTICAL STUDIES
IN THE NEW TESTAMENT DOCTRINE OF PERSONAL
SANCTIFICATION (London: Marshall, Morgan &
Scott, 1967). Summarizing and reformulating
in his lucid style, he observes, OUR HIGH
CALLING, p. 194, that sanctification, "is a
continuous inward renewing by the Divine Spir-
it, with a view to the transfiguration of

of character." All subsequent work will need
to begin with Baxter.

There have been several works which have en-
deavored to express "the Keswick Position" on
the issues of sin, consecration and sanctifi-
cation. The earliest was THE KESWICK LIBRARY,
including works by many prominent Keswick per-
sonalities. Published by Marshall Brothers,
London, the LIBRARY consisted of: G. H. C.
MacGregor, THE HOLY LIFE; F. S. Webster, THE
SECRET OF HOLINESS; Evan H. Hopkins, HIDDEN,
YET POSSESSED; F. B. Meyer, CALVARY TO PENTE-
COST; Hubert Brooke, "THEY MIGHT BE." Jer.
xiii.11; E. W. Moore, THE LIFE OF FELLOWSHIP;
J. T. Wrenford, REALITY; Lucy Bennett, LIFTED
LOADS; W. Houghton, THE SECRET OF POWER FOR
DAILY LIVING; Sophia M. Nugent, "INSTEAD;"
C. A. Fox,[52] VICTORY THROUGH THE NAME; C. G.
Moore, "THINGS WHICH CANNOT BE SHAKEN." This
LIBRARY, published 1894-1895, wielded consid-
erable influence and individual volumes have
been reprinted.

Charles Harford's anthology, THE KESWICK CON-
VENTION (London: Marshall Bros.), published
in 1907, as the torch of leadership was being
passed from the founding fathers to the second generation, contains a concise summary
of the Keswick "message," written by H. C. G.
Moule, Hubert Brooke, A. T. Pierson and J. B.
Figgis. A. T. Pierson, FORWARD MOVEMENTS OF
THE LAST HALF CENTURY (New York: Funk & Wagnalls, 1900), is also significant, chapter 3
being devoted to "Keswick Teaching," chapter
4 to "Keswick Method."

----

52. Fox, a prominent early Keswick leader,
has been the subject of studies by Barabas, SO GREAT SALVATION and by Sophia M. Nugent, CHARLES ARMSTRONG FOX: MEMORIALS (London: Marshall Bros., 1901). For his role in
Keswick, see also J. C. Pollock, THE KESWICK
STORY.

Nothing, however, has had an impact comparable to Herbert F. Stevenson's four anthologies. The earliest, KESWICK'S AUTHENTIC VOICE (1959), and KESWICK'S TRIUMPHANT VOICE (1963), published by Zondervan, contain addresses delivered at the Keswick Convention from its earliest days. Both are organized around the foci: (1) Sin in the believer, (2) God's remedy for sin, (3) Consecration, and (4) The Spirit-filled life. Later collections, THE MINISTRY OF KESWICK: A SELECTION FROM THE BIBLE READINGS DELIVERED AT THE KESWICK CONVENTION, FIRST SERIES 1892-1919 (1963), and SECOND SERIES: 1921-1956 (1964), published by Zondervan, use similar categories for organization of material. These volumes provide significant information about Keswickian teaching.

Two additional aspects of Christian doctrine have been sporadically prominent, faith healing and eschatology, both having received more attention in American than in British circles. In America, A. J. Gordon, THE MINISTRY OF HEALING: OR, MIRACLES OF CURE IN ALL AGES (New York: Revell, 1882), reprinted in 1961 by Christian Publications, aroused widespread interest. Andrew Murray, DIVINE HEALING (New York: Christian Alliance, 1900), was reprinted in slightly altered form by Christian Literature Crusade in 1971. David Caradog Jones, SPIRITUAL HEALING: AN OBJECTIVE STUDY OF A PERENNIAL GRACE (London: Longmans, Green, 1955), is less than objective in its enthusiastic analysis. Jessie Penn-Lewis, of Welsh revival fame, contributed SOUL AND SPIRIT: A GLIMPSE INTO BIBLICAL PSYCHOLOGY (Bournemouth: Overcomer Book Room, n.d.). S. D. Gordon, QUIET TALKS ABOUT THE HEALING CHRIST (New York: Revell, 1924), is a study of "some principles of healing as taught in God's Word, directly and indirectly" (p. 5). Admiral E. Gardiner Fishbourne, WHOLENESS: OR, HOLINESS AND HEALTH THROUGH FAITH IN THE LORD JESUS CHRIST (London:

Stock, 1882), is prefaced by an essay "Faith Healing No New Doctrine" by Asa Mahan who argues that healing has long been a reputable practice within the church.

Efforts in analysis of the eschaton among early Keswick leaders consisted primarily of sermons, such as, H. W. Webb-Peploe, HE COMETH! (London: Marshall Bros., 1905), J. Stuart Holden, "BEHOLD, HE COMETH!" ADDRESSES ON THE SECOND COMING OF OUR LORD (London: Morgan & Scott, 1918), and H. C. G. Moule, CHRIST'S WITNESS TO THE LIFE TO COME AND OTHER SERMONS (London: Seeley, 1908). These, as the more sophisticated study of R. W. Dale, CHRIST AND THE FUTURE LIFE (4th ed. London: Hodder & Stoughton, 1902), are in continuity with the traditional understanding of the Christian church. More heavily influenced by the burgeoning enthusiasm for dispensationalism[53] were G. Campbell Morgan, GOD'S METHODS WITH MAN IN TIME: PAST, PRESENT, AND FUTURE (New York: Revell, 1898), complete with folded colored chart!; SUNRISE. "BEHOLD, HE COMETH!" AN INTRODUCTION TO A STUDY OF THE SECOND ADVENT (New York: Revell, 1912), originally preached as sermons; and William Graham Scroggie, RULING LINES OF PROGRESSIVE REVELATION (London: Marshall Bros., 1918). Also of interest is Herbert Stewart, THE STRONGHOLD OF PROPHECY: IRREFUTABLE EVIDENCE FROM FULFILLED PROPHECY THAT THE SCRIPTURES

---

53. Essential for understanding the complex matrix of millenarian dispensationalism of the early twentieth century is Ernest Sandeen, THE ROOTS OF FUNDAMENTALISM: BRITISH AND AMERICAN MILLENARIANISM, 1800-1930 (Chicago: Univ. of Chicago, 1969). Also helpful, primarily for bibliographies and for summaries of positions is Arnold D. Ehlert, A BIBLIOGRAPHIC HISTORY OF DISPENSATIONALISM (Grand Rapids: Baker, 1965).

ARE THE INFALLIBLE WORD OF GOD (London: Marshall, Morgan & Scott, 1935), endorsed by R.
H. Stephens Richardson, Chairman of the North
Ireland (Keswick) Convention, which begins
with a lengthy quotation from C. I. Scofield.

Moody's heirs, perhaps more than Moody himself, have influenced every aspect of American religious life and thought. The higher
life movement of which he was the most spectacular example has to a great extent defined what are the accepted patterns of
thought and behavior for the typical conservative American Christian. This phenomenon
can be considered here only as it revolves
around The Moody Bible Institute. There are,
however, a myriad of Bible schools, institutes, Bible training centers, denominations,
colleges and associations which espouse the
Moody model. Although perhaps not its most
enthusiastic participant, MBI has provided a
seed-bed for the "Evangelical Awakening" of
the second half of the twentieth century.

Moody himself wrote two volumes which present
a Keswickian understanding of sanctification,
both published in Chicago by Revell: SECRET
POWER: OR, THE SECRET OF SUCCESS IN CHRIS-
TIAN LIFE AND CHRISTIAN WORK (1881), often
reprinted and, THE WAY TO GOD AND HOW TO FIND
IT (1884).   R. A. Torrey,recipient of Moody's
"mantle," wrote extensively on the Spirit-
directed life. THE BAPTISM WITH THE HOLY
SPIRIT (New York: Revell, 1895), is thoroughly Keswickian rather than Wesleyan, progressive rather than crisis-oriented in emphasis.
HOW TO OBTAIN FULNESS OF POWER IN CHRISTIAN
LIFE AND SERVICE (London: Nisbet, 1897), is
a study designed for laymen, while the fol-
lowing are more technical in expression: THE
HOLY SPIRIT, WHO HE IS AND WHAT HE DOES AND
HOW TO KNOW HIM IN ALL THE FULNESS OF HIS GRA-
CIOUS AND GLORIOUS MINISTRY (New York: Re-
vell, 1927), and THE PERSON AND WORK OF THE
HOLY SPIRIT AS REVEALED IN THE SCRIPTURES AND

IN PERSONAL EXPERIENCE (New York: Revell, 1910), reprinted by Zondervan.

Ironside's anti-Wesleyan-Holiness polemic, HOLINESS, THE FALSE AND THE TRUE has been mentioned. More positive is THE MISSION OF THE HOLY SPIRIT; AND, PRAYING IN THE HOLY SPIRIT (combined ed.: New York: Loizeaux Bros., 1950). Although not directly associated with Moody Church or Moody Bible Institute, James H. McConkey, THE THREE-FOLD SECRET OF THE HOLY SPIRIT (Pittsburgh, Pa.: Silver, 1897), reprinted by Moody, was well received and translated into at least twenty languages. McConkey was an able tractarian. His best are THE ABUNDANT LIFE, GUIDANCE, and LAW AND GRACE, still available from "Back to the Bible," Lincoln, Nebraska. A close friend of McConkey, Robert C. McQuilkin, published "What is Pentecost's Message Today?" in THE SUNDAY SCHOOL TIMES and later reprinted it as

THE BAPTISM OF THE SPIRIT: SHALL WE SEEK IT? (Columbia, S. C.: Columbia Bible College, 1935), which attacks both Pentecostalism and "dead orthodoxy." William Culbertson, president of Moody Bible Institute and speaker at both American and British Keswick conventions, has contributed GOD'S PROVISION FOR HOLY LIVING (Chicago: Moody, 1957), and THE FAITH ONCE DELIVERED (Chicago: Moody, 1972).

An intense concern of the American higher life movement, however, was eschatology and prophecy. Sandeen, ROOTS OF FUNDAMENTALISM, chronicles the development of millenarianism and the role of Keswickians, Moody and Scofield within that movement. C. I. Scofield, founder of Dallas Theological Seminary, was the synthesizer of this material in the SCOFIELD BIBLE. See also his ADDRESSES ON PROPHECY (New York: Gaebelein, 1910).

H. A. Ironside, THE LAMP OF PROPHECY, OR SIGNS OF THE TIMES (Grand Rapids: Zondervan, 1940), followed Scofield's outline while en-

deavoring to avoid extreme positions. Also
dispensational in nature was Donald Grey Barnhouse, TEACHING THE WORD OF TRUTH (Philadelphia: Revelation Book Service, 1940). More
recently, Wilbur M. Smith, YOU CAN KNOW THE
FUTURE (Glendale, Calif.: Regal Books, 1971),
and J. Dwight Pentecost, WILL MAN SURVIVE?
and PROPHECY FOR TODAY, along with the European scholar René Pache, THE FUTURE LIFE,
translated by Helen I. Needham (Chicago:
Moody, 1962),have been influential in this
area.

A. B. Simpson, THE FOUR-FOLD GOSPEL (New York:
Christian Alliance, 1890), reprinted with introduction by F. H. Senft in 1925, placed in
perspective the four-fold theological emphases of the Christian and Missionary Alliance:
the proclamation of Christ as Saviour, Sanctifier, Healer and Coming King.

Regarding Christ as Saviour, see A. B. Simp-
son, THE NAMES OF JESUS (New York: Christian
Alliance, 1892), and THE FULNESS OF JESUS; OR,
CHRISTIAN LIFE IN THE NEW TESTAMENT (New York:
Christian Alliance, 1890). The Keswickian al-
ternative of sanctification[54] was predominant
in the writings of A. B. Simpson, G. P.
Pardington, A. W. Tozer and Oswald J. Smith.
Simpson accomplished a major study, THE HOLY
SPIRIT: OR, POWER FROM ON HIGH, AN UNFOLDING
OF THE DOCTRINE OF THE HOLY SPIRIT IN THE OLD
AND NEW TESTAMENTS (2 vols.; New York: The
Christian Alliance, 1896). WHOLLY SANCTIFIED
and A LARGER CHRISTIAN LIFE are more system-
atic presentations of his views which were
reformulated by George P. Pardington, THE
CRISIS OF THE DEEPER LIFE.

---

54. The Wesleyan understanding of entire
    sanctification still has support in the
C. & M. A., probably because of its continuing contacts with the HOLINESS MOVEMENT and

Aiden Wilson Tozer, Simpson's successor, has
published several items about the holy life
(published by Christian Publications, Harris-
burg, except where otherwise noted): KEYS TO
THE DEEPER LIFE from the series in CHRISTIAN
LIFE (Grand Rapids: Zondervan, 1957); OF GOD
AND MEN (1960), in non-technical format; HOW
TO BE FILLED WITH THE HOLY SPIRIT, a series
of sermons; and THE KNOWLEDGE OF THE HOLY;
THE ATTRIBUTES OF GOD: THEIR MEANING IN
CHRISTIAN LIFE (New York: Harper, 1961), his
most famous work. Also sermonic is THE ROOT
OF THE RIGHTEOUS (1955).

Oswald J. Smith, founder and longtime pastor
of the famed Peoples Church of Toronto, Canada, is a prolific writer. His best materials focusing upon the issue of sanctification
are THE ENDUEMENT OF POWER (1933), revised in
1962, THE SPIRIT AT WORK (1939) and THE LORD
IS CALLING (1937), all published by Marshall,
Morgan & Scott, London.

Christ, the Healer, was the focus of A. J.
Gordon, MINISTRY OF HEALING which led Simpson
to an experience of healing and the writing
of THE DISCOVERY OF HEALING,THE GOSPEL OF
HEALING and LORD FOR THE BODY. Oswald J.
Smith, THE GREAT PHYSICIAN (New York: Chris-
tian Alliance, 1927), and Thomas J. McCrossan,
BODILY HEALING AND THE ATONEMENT (Seattle:
McCrossan, 1930), also reflect the concern
for healing.

A. B. Simpson, THE GOSPEL OF THE KINGDOM (2nd
ed.; 1890) is a vaguely premillennialist anal-
ysis based on a series of sermons, as is HEAV-
EN OPENED: EXPOSITIONS OF THE BOOK OF REVELA-
TION, in the CHRIST IN THE BIBLE series, Vol.
XXIV (1899). EPISTLES OF THE ADVENT; OR, THE

---

the number of clergy who have attended Asbury
College and Asbury Theological Seminary.

BLESSED HOPE IN THESSALONIANS (n.d.) and THE
COMING ONE (1912) are biblical-theological
studies, while more allegorical is BACK TO
PATMOS; OR, PROPHETIC OUTLOOK ON PRESENT CON-
DITIONS (1914). All these were published by
the Christian Alliance, now Christian Publications, Harrisburg, Pennsylvania.

George Palmer Pardington, the best theologian
of the Christian & Missionary Alliance em-
phasized a pre-millennial dispensationalist ap-
proach in OUTLINE STUDIES IN CHRISTIAN DOC-
TRINE (New York: Christian Alliance, 1916).
Oswald J. Smith, with more enthusiasm than
discretion published IS THE ANTICHRIST AT
HAND? (3rd ed., Toronto: Tabernacle Publish-
ers, 1926), an analysis of Mussolini; and
WHEN THE KING COMES BACK (London: Marshall,
Morgan & Scott, 1957), with an introduction
by Wilbur M. Smith, who himself wrote, WORLD
CRISES AND THE PROPHETIC SCRIPTURES (Chicago:
Moody, 1950), all now hopelessly out of date!
Oswald J. Smith, THE CLOUDS ARE LIFTING,
(n.d.), studies in prophecy and the visions
of Daniel, and PROPHECY - WHAT LIES AHEAD?
(1943, 1945, 1947, 1952), both published by
Marshall, Morgan & Scott, are more cautious
in prognostication and analogy.

For bibliographical hints concerning the theological perspective of the Pentecostals and
the Holiness Movement see Faupel, THE AMERI-
CAN PENTECOSTAL MOVEMENT and Dayton, THE AMER-
ICAN HOLINESS MOVEMENT. Within Methodism the
trend of the twentieth century was away from
a Wesleyan perfectionist understanding and toward a Keswickian perception of sanctification. Exemplary of this move is James Mudge,[55]

---

55. Mudge's own "testimony" appears in FORTY
    WITNESSES, COVERING THE WHOLE RANGE OF
CHRISTIAN EXPERIENCE, edited by S. Olin Garrison (New York: Hunt & Eaton, 1888). More

GROWTH IN HOLINESS TOWARD PERFECTION: OR,
PROGRESSIVE SANCTIFICATION (1895), which was
viciously attacked by the perfectionist stal-
wart, Daniel Steele, A DEFENSE OF CHRISTIAN
PERFECTION: OR, A CRITICISM OF DR. JAMES
MUDGE'S "GROWTH IN HOLINESS TOWARD PERFECTION"
(1896), and by Lewis Romaine Dunn, A MANUAL
OF HOLINESS AND REVIEW OF DR. JAMES B. MUDGE
(1895). Mudge replied by, THE PERFECT LIFE
IN EXPERIENCE AND DOCTRINE: A RESTATEMENT,
WITH INTRODUCTION BY REV. WILLIAM F. WARREN
(1911). All these titles were published in
New York by Hunt & Eaton or Eaton & Mains,
and in Cincinnati by Cranston & Curts, et al.

Alexander Alonzo Phelps, PURITY AND POWER: OR,
THE TWELVE P'S, A RADICAL AND SCRIPTURAL
TREATMENT OF THE DOCTRINE, EXPERIENCE AND
PRACTICE OF CHRISTIAN PERFECTION (Boston: Ad-
vent Christian, 1905), is a work by a Metho-
dist Episcopal writer who draws upon and rec-
ommends both the perfectionist holiness and
Keswickian writings of Daniel Steele and F.
B. Meyer.

Biblical Studies

Participants at the Keswick Convention have
been predominantly pastors, evangelists, missionaries, and Bible school faculty, rather
than academicians. This fact is reflected in
the biblical studies of Keswick men. These
works were seldom seminal, but served to en-
courage a greater degree of personal Bible
study or to indicate support for their theological perspective--at a lay level. The effectiveness of this approach may be seen by
the wide distribution the literature has received, and by the extensive support their
critical-theological positions have received

---

technical biographical data may be traced
through Jones, A GUIDE TO THE STUDY OF THE
HOLINESS MOVEMENT, p. 707.

from laity and clergy of all denominations in England and America.

The philosophical concepts controlling their exposition can be found in W. Graham Scroggie, IS THE BIBLE THE WORD OF GOD? (Philadelphia: Sunday School Times, 1922), answered affirmatively in the outline: "It seems to be; It claims to be; It proves to be." Scroggie delivered Bible readings at the Keswick Convention twelve times. Hubert Brooke, "Is the Bible Inspired?" in CAN WE TRUST THE BIBLE? CHAPTERS ON BIBLICAL CRITICISM (London: The Religious Tract Society, 1908), pps. 1-35, defended his thesis by analysis of prophecy and personal experience. A. T. Pierson, THE BIBLE AND SPIRITUAL CRITICISM (New York: Baker & Taylor, 1905), delivered first as the Exeter Hall Lectures on the Bible, is a defense of what would become the Fundamentalist approach to scripture. W. H. Griffith Thomas, "Old Testament Criticism and New Testament Christianity," in BACK TO THE BIBLE: THE TRIUMPHS OF TRUTH, by A. C. Dixon, et al. (London: Partridge, 1912), pp. 77-102, maintains that "the old is better" in response to the newly-arrived-in-America higher criticism.

No one was a more severe critic of higher criticism than R. A. Torrey, who for that reason was chosen by Moody to preside over the Chicago (later, Moody) Bible Institute. DIFFICULTIES AND ALLEGED ERRORS AND CONTRADICTIONS IN THE BIBLE (New York: Revell, 1907), TEN REASONS WHY I BELIEVE THE BIBLE IS THE WORD OF GOD (Chicago: Bible Inst. Colportage Assn., 1898), and especially THE HIGHER CRITICISM AND THE NEW THEOLOGY: UNSCIENTIFIC, UNSCRIPTURAL, AND UNWHOLESOME (Montrose, Pa.: Montrose Christian Literature Soc., 1911), defined the American Keswickian approach to scripture. As is obvious from the authors cited, the nature of scripture was a far greater issue in America than in Britain, and continues to be so. René Pache, THE INSPIRA-

TION AND AUTHORITY OF SCRIPTURE, translated by
Helen I. Needham (Chicago: Moody, 1969), continues in the same tradition.

A. T. Pierson, THE BIBLE AND SPIRITUAL LIFE
(London: Nisbet, 1908), is an effort to show
the practical nature of the scripture and the
virtue of personal Bible study. The emphasis
of Keswick on both sides of the Atlantic has
been to study the text as it stands rather
than to engage in higher criticism. This has
led to "How to" manuals exemplified by R. A.
Torrey, HOW TO STUDY THE BIBLE FOR GREATEST
PROFIT (London: Nisbet, 1896); THE IMPOR-
TANCE AND VALUE OF PROPER BIBLE STUDY (Chica-
go: Moody, 1921); THE NEW TOPICAL TEXT BOOK;
A SCRIPTURE TEXT BOOK FOR THE USE OF MINIS-
TERS, TEACHERS, AND ALL CHRISTIAN WORKERS.
WITH AN INTRODUCTION ON METHODS OF BIBLE STU-
DY BY REV.R. A. TORREY (New York: Revell,
1897); and introductions to the Bible such as
W. Graham Scroggie, 56 KNOW YOUR BIBLE, A
BRIEF INTRODUCTION TO THE SCRIPTURES, 2 vols.
(London: Pickering & Inglis, 1940; revised
1953; often reprinted), Scroggie, THE UNFOLD-
ING DRAMA OF REDEMPTION; THE BIBLE AS A WHOLE,
3 vols. (London: Pickering & Inglis, 1953-
1970), is a "synthetic" approach, interpret-
ing the Bible as one integral unit.

The commentator par excellence was William
Henry Griffith Thomas, whose work greatly influenced evangelical Anglicanism as well as
the Keswick Convention. On a methodological

---

56. W. G. Scroggie still holds the record
for Bible readings at the Keswick Convention: twelve between 1914 and 1954. THE
STORY OF A LIFE IN THE LOVE OF GOD, incidents
collected from the diaries of Mrs. James J.
(Jane) Scroggie and edited by her son, Dr. W.
Graham Scroggie (London: Pickering & Inglis,
1939) provides insights to Scroggie himself.

level are HOW WE GOT OUR BIBLE AND WHY WE BE-
LIEVE IT IS GOD'S WORD (Chicago: Moody,
1926), METHODS OF BIBLE STUDY (Chicago: Bible Inst. Colportage Assn., 1924), and HOW TO
STUDY THE FOUR GOSPELS (Philadelphia: Sunday
School Times, 1924). Thomas contributed the
following to A DEVOTIONAL COMMENTARY SERIES,
edited by A. R. Buckland and published by the
Religious Tract Society, London: GENESIS, 3
vols., reprinted as one volume (Grand Rapids:
Eerdmans, 1946), ROMANS, 3 vols. (reprinted
as one volume by Eerdmans, 1946), dedicated
to H. C. G. Moule, who contributed the volume, II TIMOTHY to the same series. Much of
the material of Thomas, THE ACTS OF THE APOS-
TLES: OUTLINE STUDIES IN PRIMITIVE CHRIS-
TIANITY (Chicago: Moody, 1939), was incorporated in OUTLINE STUDIES IN THE ACTS OF THE
APOSTLES (Eerdmans, 1956), edited by his
daughter who also edited his OUTLINE STUDIES
IN THE GOSPEL OF LUKE (Eerdmans, 1950), and
THROUGH THE PENTATEUCH CHAPTER BY CHAPTER
(Eerdmans, 1957).

Influential since the early era of the Conven-
tion has been H. C. G. Moule, THE EPISTLE OF
ST. PAUL TO THE ROMANS, EXPOSITOR'S BIBLE
SERIES (London: Hodder & Stoughton, 1894),
often reprinted, and the more scholarly vol-
ume in "The Cambridge Bible for Schools and
Colleges," THE EPISTLE OF PAUL THE APOSTLE TO
THE ROMANS (Cambridge: Univ. Press, 1899).

W. G. Scroggie commented on THE PSALMS, 4
vols. (London: Pickering & Inglis, 1948).
On the Acts of Apostles, commentaries were of-
fered by A. T. Pierson, THE ACTS OF THE HOLY
SPIRIT, dedicated to A. J. Gordon (London:
Marshall, Morgan & Scott, 1913), G. Campbell
Morgan, THE ACTS OF THE APOSTLES (New York:
Revell, 1924), and A. Q. Morton and G. H. C.
MacGregor, THE STRUCTURE OF LUKE AND ACTS
(New York: Harper & Row, 1964). On Romans,
in addition to those mentioned above, there
are commentaries by A. B. Simpson, THE EPIS-

TLE TO THE ROMANS (Harrisburg, Pa.: Christian Publications, n.d.), and Robert C. McQuilkin, THE MESSAGE OF ROMANS: AN EXPOSITION (Grand Rapids: Zondervan, 1947).

The Keswickians have been prolific and good Bible expositors. H. A. Ironside has published, through Loizeaux Brothers, notes on Proverbs, Ezra, Nehemiah, Esther, Jeremiah and Lamentations, the Minor Prophets, Daniel, the Revelation and Philippians, all of which have gone through several printings. F. B. Meyer published expositions on most books of the Bible. There is not space to list all of them. The best is THE EPISTLE TO THE PHILIPPIANS: A DEVOTIONAL COMMENTARY (London: Religious Tract Society, 1906). More recent are the works of John R. W. Stott, THE EPISTLES OF JOHN, TYNDALE NEW TESTAMENT COMMENTARIES, Vol. 19 (Grand Rapids: Eerdmans, 1964), THE MESSAGE OF GALATIANS (London: Inter-Varsity , 1968), GUARD THE GOSPEL: THE MESSAGE OF II TIMOTHY (Downers Grove, Ill.: Inter-Varsity, 1973), and Herbert F. Stevenson, THREE PROPHETIC VOICES: STUDIES IN JOEL, AMOS, AND HOSEA (1971), and JAMES SPEAKS FOR TODAY (1966),both by Marshall, Morgan & Scott.

Still less technical are numerous Bible addresses. Sir Stevenson Arthur Blackwood,[57] HEAVENLY PLACES. ADDRESSES ON THE BOOK OF JOSHUA (London: Nisbet, 1872), and THINGS WHICH GOD HATH JOINED TOGETHER: ADDRESSES ON ISAIAH XLV. 21-25 (London: Nisbet, 1878); Charles A. Fox, THE SPIRITUAL GRASP OF THE EPISTLES; OR, AN EPISTLE A-SUNDAY (London: Partridge, 1894); George Goodman, THE EPISTLE OF ETERNAL LIFE: AN EXPOSITION OF THE FIRST EPISTLE OF JOHN (London: Pickering & Inglis, 1936); A. T. Pierson, HIS FULNESS: FOUR BI-

---

57. Blackwood was one of Robert Pearsall Smith's supporters who became a leading Keswick Convention personality. See Lady

BLE READINGS GIVEN AT KESWICK IN 1904 ON I
CORINTHIANS I.30 (London: Marshall Bros.,
1904); and W. H. Griffith Thomas, "LET US GO
ON:" THE SECRET OF CHRISTIAN PROGRESS IN THE
EPISTLE TO THE HEBREWS (London: Morgan &
Scott, 1923). The best of the Bible readings
at the Keswick Convention have been edited by
H. F. Stevenson in THE MINISTRY OF KESWICK.

Sermonic and Devotional Studies

The greatest contribution of the Keswick Convention and the higher life movement has been
the literature explicating Christian spirituality or devotional literature. Almost every
Keswick speaker of note has published a volume of sermons, the largest collection being
that of G. Campbell Morgan, THE WESTMINSTER
PULPIT, 10 vols. (New York: Revell, 1954-
1955), with a topical-textual index published
separately in 1954. THE TOZER PULPIT, 5 vols.
to date, edited and compiled by Gerald B.
Smith (Harrisburg, Pa.: Christian Publications, 1968-), is a major effort to preserve
the sermons of the great Christian and Missionary Alliance preacher. THE KESWICK WEEK
prints annually the sermons, Bible readings
and homilies delivered at the Keswick Convention.

According to some canons of evaluation, all
of the literature discussed above might be
considered "devotional." In a sense that is
true for the goal of Keswick, "the promotion
of practical holiness"--always somewhat intro-
spective--has resulted in a richness of spiritual roadmaps for progress in Christian maturity. To list all literature would be far
beyond the scope of this essay, and to assert
that those mentioned below are the best would

Stevenson Arthur Blackwood, SOME RECORDS OF
THE LIFE OF STEVENSON ARTHUR BLACKWOOD, K. C.
B. (London: Hodder & Stoughton, 1896).

be imprudent. Therefore, the method of this section is to introduce the reader to devotional literature by several of the more prominent Keswickian writers. A more extensive list may be found in Barabas, SO GREAT SALVATION.

From the preludes of Keswick, Hannah Whitall Smith, THE CHRISTIAN'S SECRET OF A HAPPY LIFE has retained popularity witnessed by the frequent reprintings by Revell. Early Keswick leaders produced devotional literature of enduring attraction: S. D. Gordon authored the popular series, QUIET TALKS, at least 23 volumes, published by Revell; Alexander Smellie, SERVICE AND INSPIRATION and THE WELL BY THE WAY (London: Melrose, 1904 and 1920); Charles A. Fox, VICTORY THROUGH THE NAME (1894); and H. W. Webb-Peploe, "I FOLLOW AFTER" (1894), WITHIN AND WITHOUT: OR, THE CHRISTIAN'S FOES (1900), the last three published by Marshall Bros., and THE LIFE OF PRIVILEGE, POSSESSION, PEACE, AND POWER (London: Nisbet, 1896).

H. C. G. Moule, the scholar, preacher, bishop, produced CHRIST AND THE CHRISTIAN: WORDS SPOKEN AT KESWICK (London: Marshall Bros., 1919), THE CROSS AND THE SPIRIT (London: Seeley, 1898), and SECRET PRAYER (London: Seeley, 1890). Perhaps no one has been more influential in Keswickian spirituality, though he spoke only once at the Convention, than Andrew Murray who wrote among other things, THE MASTER'S INDWELLING, (1896) and THE INNER CHAMBER AND THE INNER LIFE (1905) both by Revell, THE SCHOOL OF OBEDIENCE (London: Nisbet, 1898), and ABIDE IN CHRIST: THOUGHTS ON THE BLESSED LIFE OF FELLOWSHIP WITH THE SON OF GOD (London: Nisbet, 1883). Many of Murray's works are being reprinted, as indicated in recent editions of BOOKS IN PRINT.

F. B. Meyer, CHRISTIAN LIVING (London: Morgan & Scott, 1888), and THE DIRECTORY OF THE

DEVOUT LIFE: MEDITATIONS ON THE SERMON ON
THE MOUNT (New York: Revell, 1904), continue
to sustain interest while the once popular
writings of W. H. M. H. Aitken, especially
THE HIGHWAY OF HOLINESS: HELPS TO THE SPIRIT-
UAL LIFE (London: Shaw, 1883), unfortunately
do not. G. H. C. MacGregor, "RABBONI:" OR,
PERSONAL CONSECRATION (London: Marshall Bros.,
1904), and A HOLY LIFE AND HOW TO LIVE IT
(London: Marshall, Morgan & Scott, 1894),
are complements to the more erudite work of
an able scholar.

Jessie Penn-Lewis, of Welsh revival fame was
a popular author of devotional literature.
THE CROSS OF CALVARY AND ITS MESSAGE (London:
Marshall Bros., 1903), has gone through eight
editions, and OPENED HEAVENS (Parkstone: Overcomer Literature Trust, n.d.), has been recently reprinted.

The Fleming H. Revell Company published two
significant devotional series around the turn
of the century. LITTLE BOOKS FOR LIFE'S GUID-
ANCE included writings such as G. Campbell
Morgan, DISCIPLESHIP; Andrew Murray, THE
LORD'S TABLE; F. B. Meyer, SAVED AND KEPT,
COUNSELS TO YOUNG BELIEVERS, CHEER FOR LIFE'S
PILGRIMAGE; J. H. Barrows, I BELIEVE IN GOD
THE FATHER ALMIGHTY; and A. J. Gordon, YET
SPEAKING, UNPUBLISHED ADDRESSES. THE NORTH-
FIELD SERIES, addresses delivered at Moody's
Northfield Convention included G. Campbell
Morgan, THE TRUE ESTIMATE OF LIFE AND HOW TO
LIVE. Horatius Bonar, HOW SHALL I GO TO GOD
and GOD'S WAY OF PEACE, D. L. Moody, WEIGHED
AND WANTING: THE TEN COMMANDMENTS, as well
as other authors.

Amy Wilson Carmichael, the Keswick Convention's first missionary, continues to charm
Christian readers. EDGES OF HIS WAYS; SELEC-
TIONS FOR DAILY READING (London: S.P.C.K.,
1955); GOLD BY MOONLIGHT (London: S.P.C.K.,
1935); a book of meditations, IF... (London:

S.P.C.K., 1938); THOU GIVEST...THEY GATHER
(Fort Washington, Pa.: Christian Literature
Crusade, 1958); and the often reprinted WIN-
DOWS (London: S.P.C.K., 1937), are popular
devotional reading.

Devotional writings of other Keswick conven-
tioners are: Theodore Monod, THE GIFT OF GOD
(1876); W. Y. Fullerton, THE PRACTICE OF
CHRIST'S PRESENCE (1916), and GOD'S INTENTION
(1931); and Lionel B. Fletcher, AFTER CONVER-
SION - WHAT? (1936), all published by Marshall, Morgan & Scott, London; W. H. Griffith
Thomas, THE CHRISTIAN LIFE AND HOW TO LIVE IT
(Chicago: Moody, 1919); Gordon Watt, THE
CROSS IN FAITH AND CONDUCT (Philadelphia: Sunday School Times, 1922). Major W. Ian Thomas,
prominent in American and British Keswick circles, THE SAVING LIFE OF CHRIST (Grand Rapids:
Zondervan, 1961), is a popular study in the
atonement.

188

The American Keswickians were also prolific
writers of devotional literature. R. A. Tor-
rey, HOW TO SUCCEED IN THE CHRISTIAN LIFE
(1906), and REAL SALVATION AND WHOLEHEARTED
SERVICE (1905), as well as Robert Speer's ad-
dresses at Northfield, "REMEMBER JESUS CHRIST"
AND OTHER TALKS ABOUT CHRIST AND THE CHRIS-
TIAN LIFE (1899), were all published by Re-
vell. A. T. Pierson authored CATHARINE OF
SIENA, AN ANCIENT LAY PREACHER; A STORY OF
SANCTIFIED WOMANHOOD AND POWER IN PRAYER (New
York: Funk & Wagnalls, 1898), as well as the
more traditional THE BELIEVER'S LIFE: ITS
PAST, PRESENT, AND FUTURE TENSES (London:
Morgan & Scott, 1905).

James H. McConkey,[58] the founder of Silver

----

58. Louise Harrison McCraw, McConkey's long-
     time secretary, has written JAMES H. MC-
CONKEY, A MAN OF GOD (2nd ed., Grand Rapids:
Zondervan, 1939; reprinted Three Hills, Al-

Publishing Company, a non-profit press, pub-
lished THE THREE-FOLD SECRET OF THE HOLY SPIR-
IT, discussed above, and devotional tracts,
FAITH, GUIDANCE, CHASTENING, PRAYER, PRAYER
AND HEALING and GIVE GOD A CHANCE, all of
which are in print with Back to the Bible
Broadcast of Lincoln, Nebraska.

Stephen Olford, MANNA IN THE MORNING (1969)
and THE SECRET OF STRENGTH (1973)(Chicago:
Moody), the size of which belies their
influence, have had wide circulation. Alan
Redpath published sermons and abstracts of
sermons preached while he was pastor of Moody
Memorial Church, Chicago: LEARNING TO LIVE
(Grand Rapids: Eerdmans, 1961), and BLESS-
INGS OUT OF BUFFETINGS, STUDIES IN II CORIN-
THIANS (Westwood, N. J.: Revell, 1965).
Donald Grey Barnhouse, an American evangelist
who spoke several times at the Keswick Conven-
tion, wrote the popular GOD'S METHODS FOR
HOLY LIVING: PRACTICAL LESSONS IN EXPERIMEN-   **189**
TAL HOLINESS (London: Pickering & Inglis,
1937), THE INVISIBLE WAR (Grand Rapids: Zon-
dervan, 1965), and LIFE BY THE SON; PRACTICAL
LESSONS IN EXPERIMENTAL HOLINESS (Philadel-
phia: Revelation Publications, American Bible Conf. Assn., 1939).

Oswald J. Smith and the Christian and Missionary Alliance writers, Simpson and Tozer, contributed significantly to devotional literature in addition to their other works. Simpson wrote WALKING IN THE SPIRIT: THE HOLY
SPIRIT IN CHRISTIAN EXPERIENCE, (n.d.), THE
LIFE OF PRAYER, THE SELF LIFE AND THE CHRIST
LIFE (1897) and IN HEAVENLY PLACES (1892) all
by Christian Alliance Publishing Company and
currently available from Christian Publications, Harrisburg, Pa., as are over forty other volumes by this prolific author.

---

berta; Prairie Bible Institute, 1965).

Tozer, THE PURSUIT OF GOD (1948), THAT IN-
CREDIBLE CHRISTIAN (1964), and MAN, THE DWELL-
ING PLACE OF GOD (1966), are collections of
previously published devotional pieces (Har-
risburg, Christian Publications). Oswald J.
Smith contributed FROM DEATH TO LIFE, and THE
SPIRIT FILLED LIFE (New York: Christian Al-
liance, 1925 and 1926).

Catherine Marshall, BEYOND OURSELVES (1961)
consciously attempts to update the work of
Hannah Whitall Smith. SOMETHING MORE (1974)
is also an expression of higher life concerns.
Both are McGraw-Hill publications.

Present Keswick Convention leaders such as
Herbert F. Stevenson, THE ROAD TO THE CROSS
(London: Marshall, Morgan & Scott, 1963), A
GALAXY OF SAINTS (Revell, 1958), and John R.
W. Stott, CONFESS YOUR SINS (Phila.: Westmin-
ster, 1964), MEN MADE NEW: AN EXPOSITION OF
ROMANS 5-8 (London: Inter-Varsity, 1966),
and CHRIST THE LIBERATOR (London: Hodder &
Stoughton, 1972), are continuing in the Kes-
wick tradition.

This presentation of the Keswickian tradition
of spirituality indicates the diversity and
yet the sameness of the concern. There is
little change - merely, although importantly,
a re-stating of emphases for the Keswick audience and the Christian world.

Hymnody

The hymnody of the Keswick Convention has,
for all practical purposes, been ignored. F.
S. Webster, "Keswick Hymns," in THE KESWICK
CONVENTION, ITS MESSAGE, ITS METHOD AND ITS
MEN, edited by Charles F. Harford, is long on
glowing description and void of concrete analysis.

Initially Robert Pearsall Smith, HYMNS SELECT-
ED FROM FABER (Boston: Willard Tract Reposi-

tory; London: W. Isbister, 1874), without music, was received widely. This was replaced by HYMNS OF CONSECRATION AND FAITH: FOR USE AT GENERAL CHRISTIAN CONFERENCES, MEETINGS FOR THE DEEPENING OF SPIRITUAL LIFE AND CONSECRATION MEETINGS, compiled and arranged by Rev. J. Mountain (n.d.), of which a second edition, new and enlarged was compiled by Mrs. Evan Hopkins (1895), both published by Marshall Brothers. THE KESWICK HYMN-BOOK compiled by the Trustees of the Keswick Convention (London: Marshall, Morgan & Scott, n.d.), was published in the 1930's, followed in 1938 by an enlarged edition. Amy Carmichael published WINGS: A BOOK OF DOHNAVUR SONGS (London: S.P.C.K., 1960-).

In America, A. J. Gordon compiled THE VESTRY HYMN AND TUNE BOOK (Boston: Young, 1872). Moody's movement gave strength to American hymnody and gospel song but produced little that was distinctive. The Christian and Missionary Alliance, led by Simpson, HYMNS AND SONGS OF THE FOURFOLD GOSPEL, AND THE FULLNESS OF JESUS (New York: Christian Alliance, 1891), without music, and HYMNS OF THE CHRISTIAN LIFE; NEW AND STANDARD SONGS FOR THE SANCTUARY, SUNDAY SCHOOLS, PRAYER MEETINGS, MISSION WORK AND REVIVAL SERVICES, ed. Capt. R. Kelso Carter and Rev. A. B. Simpson (New York: Christian Alliance, 1891), with music, has since moved to a more traditional hymnal, basically indistinguishable from those of other denominations, HYMNS OF THE CHRISTIAN LIFE; A BOOK OF WORSHIP IN SONG EMPHASIZING EVANGELISM, MISSIONS AND THE DEEPER LIFE, 1936 (revised and enlarged, 1962).

Periodicals: England

THE CHRISTIAN, A WEEKLY RECORD OF CHRISTIAN LIFE, CHRISTIAN TESTIMONY AND CHRISTIAN WORK (London) 1870-1969. Here were reported the Brighton and Oxford conferences as Figgis and E. Hopkins contributed summaries. Other meetings of the Robert Pearsall Smiths received coverage as did those of Moody. There is not a complete file in the United States. From 1962 to 1969 published by The Billy Graham Evangelistic Association as THE CHRISTIAN AND CHRISTIANITY TODAY.

THE CHRISTIAN'S PATHWAY TO POWER, 1874-1878. Founded by Robert Pearsall Smith, it was, after his downfall, taken up by W. E. Boardman and then by Evan H. Hopkins. It became THE LIFE OF FAITH.

THE LIFE OF FAITH (London), 1878-   . Formerly THE CHRISTIAN'S PATHWAY TO POWER, it was supervised by Evan Hopkins, although initially edited by Charles Grandison Moore. The editorship has remained in the hands of Keswickians, and the paper remains an unofficial voice of the Keswick Convention. No complete file has been found.

KESWICK WEEK, 1892-   . The addresses delivered at the Keswick Convention have been published since 1892 under various titles. Except for the war years (1940?-1945) when these appeared as KESWICK IN LONDON or similar titles, the caption was KESWICK WEEK or KESWICK CONVENTION. Reports of conferences 1875-1891 appeared in THE LIFE OF FAITH or its predecessor THE CHRISTIAN'S PATHWAY TO POWER.

SOUTH AFRICAN PIONEER (London) 1- , 1887-

Periodicals: America

NORTHFIELD ECHOES (East Northfield, Mass.) 1-10 (1894-1903). Authors included J. W. Chapman, A. J. Gordon, Mrs. Gordon, T. S. Hamlin, F. B. Meyer, Moody, A. T. Pierson, R. A. Torrey and D. W. and M. J. Whittle.

MOODY CHURCH HERALD, (Chicago) 1902, 1903. Included articles by and about Moody, R. A.

Torrey, W. W. White and A. T. Pierson.

RECORD OF CHRISTIAN WORK (East Northfield, Mass.; 1-18 New York: Revell). 1-52 (1881-1933). Reports on the activities of Hannah Whitall Smith, Moody and Sankey, Andrew Murray and H. W. Webb-Peploe. Important are F. B. Meyer "The New Life," v. 14 (1895), 198-199 and H. W. Webb-Peploe "The True Unity of the Church," v. 15 (1896), 224-225. In April 1904 it absorbed NORTHFIELD ECHOES.

THE INSTITUTE TIE (Chicago) 1: 1-24 Nov. 7, 1891- Oct. 30, 1892; 2: 1-6, Nov. 15, 1892-Feb. 15, 1893. N.S. 1-10, 1900/01-1910. Here were published notes of R. A. Torrey's lectures at the Bible Institute as well as reports of the Moody-Sankey tours of Europe. The subtitle of the magazine varies. Complete file at Moody Bible Institute, Chicago. It became THE CHRISTIAN WORKERS MAGAZINE.

CHRISTIAN WORKERS MAGAZINE (Chicago). October, 1910-August, 1920. Complete file at Moody Bible Institute, Chicago. It became MOODY BIBLE INSTITUTE MONTHLY.

MOODY BIBLE INSTITUTE MONTHLY (Chicago). 1920-1938. Complete file at Moody Bible Institute, Chicago. It became MOODY MONTHLY.

MOODY MONTHLY (Chicago). 1938- . Complete file at Moody Bible Institute, Chicago.

THE MID-AMERICA KESWICK WEEK (Chicago). 1959. Only one published. Includes addresses by Alan Redpath, Stephen Olford, C. S. Woods, Paul Rees, Ian Thomas, Allister Smith, Arthur Matthews, H. Wildish and William Culbertson delivered at Moody Memorial Church.

MISSIONARY REVIEW OF THE WORLD (Brooklyn, N.Y.) 1878-1939. 1878-1887 was published as MISSIONARY REVIEW. Edited by A. T. Pierson. While there are no complete files, such could

be compiled. See UNION LIST OF SERIALS, III,
2692.

THE OVERCOMER (London: Bournemouth) 1909-
1914; 1920-1948. Product of the Welsh revival era, edited by Mrs. Jessie Penn-Lewis.

ADVOCATE OF CHRISTIAN HOLINESS (Boston) 1-13,
1870-1881. An American Holiness Movement
journal whose British correspondent, W. G.
Pascoe reported work of Smiths, etc. in a
column entitled, "Work of Holiness in England".
Published briefly, 1882, as ADVOCATE OF BIBLE
HOLINESS.

SOUTH AFRICAN PIONEER, American ed. (Brooklyn,
N.Y.) 1-   (Dec. 1920-   ). Aug./Sept. 1941,
merged with British edition.

Periodicals: Christian and Missionary Alliance

THE WORD, THE WORK, AND THE WORLD (New York)
1887. It became CHRISTIAN ALLIANCE AND FOR-
EIGN MISSIONARY WEEKLY.

CHRISTIAN ALLIANCE AND FOREIGN MISSIONARY
WEEKLY. 1887-1896. It became CHRISTIAN AND
MISSIONARY ALLIANCE.

CHRISTIAN AND MISSIONARY ALLIANCE. 1897-
Sept. 1911. It became ALLIANCE WEEKLY.

ALLIANCE WEEKLY. Oct. 1911-Dec. 25, 1957.
It became ALLIANCE WITNESS.

ALLIANCE WITNESS. 1957-   . Note: Volumes
24-34 are repeated in numbering.

INDEX

INDEX

INDEX

INDEX

INDEX

INDEX

INDEX

TITLES in THIS SERIES

9. RUSSELL KELSO CARTER ON "FAITH HEALING." R. Kelso Carter, *THE ATONEMENT FOR SIN AND SICKNESS* (Boston, 1884) *"FAITH HEALING" REVIEWED AFTER TWENTY YEARS* (Boston, 1897)

10. Daniels, W. H., *DR. CULLIS AND HIS WORK* (Boston, [1885])

11. HOLINESS TRACTS DEFENDING THE MINISTRY OF WOMEN. Luther Lee, *"WOMAN'S RIGHT TO PREACH THE GOSPEL; A SERMON, AT THE ORDINATION OF REV. MISS ANTOINETTE L. BROWN, AT SOUTH BUTLER, WAYNE COUNTY, N. Y., SEPT. 15, 1853"* (Syracuse, 1853) *bound with* B. T. Roberts, *ORDAINING WOMEN* (Rochester, 1891) *bound with* Catherine (Mumford) Booth, *"FEMALE MINISTRY; OR, WOMAN'S RIGHT TO PREACH THE GOSPEL . . ."* (London, n. d.) *bound with* Fannie (McDowell) Hunter, *WOMEN PREACHERS* (Dallas, 1905)

12. LATE NINETEENTH CENTURY REVIVALIST TEACHINGS ON THE HOLY SPIRIT. D. L. Moody, *SECRET POWER OR THE SECRET OF SUCCESS IN CHRISTIAN LIFE AND WORK* (New York, [1881]) *bound with* J. Wilbur Chapman, *RECEIVED YE THE HOLY GHOST?* (New York, [1894]) *bound with* R. A. Torrey, *THE BAPTISM WITH THE HOLY SPIRIT* (New York, 1895 & 1897)

13. SEVEN "JESUS ONLY" TRACTS. Andrew D. Urshan, *THE DOCTRINE OF THE NEW BIRTH, OR, THE PERFECT WAY TO ETERNAL LIFE* (Cochrane, Wis., 1921) *bound with* Andrew Urshan, *THE ALMIGHTY GOD IN THE LORD JESUS CHRIST* (Los Angeles, 1919) *bound with* Frank J. Ewart, *THE REVELATION OF JESUS CHRIST* (St. Louis, n. d.) *bound with* G. T. Haywood, *THE BIRTH OF THE SPIRIT IN THE DAYS OF THE APOSTLES* (Indianapolis, n. d.) *DIVINE NAMES AND TITLES OF JEHOVAH* (Indianapolis, n. d.) *THE FINEST OF THE WHEAT* (Indianapolis, n. d.) *THE VICTIM OF THE FLAMING SWORD* (Indianapolis, n. d.)

14. THREE EARLY PENTECOSTAL TRACTS. D. Wesley Myland, *THE LATTER RAIN COVENANT AND PENTECOSTAL POWER* (Chicago, 1910) *bound with* G. F. Taylor, *THE SPIRIT AND THE BRIDE* (n. p., [1907?]) *bound with* B. F. Laurence, *THE APOSTOLIC FAITH RESTORED* (St. Louis, 1916)

15. Fairchild, James H., *OBERLIN: THE COLONY AND THE COLLEGE, 1833-1883* (Oberlin, 1883)

16. Figgis, John B., *KESWICK FROM WITHIN* (London, [1914])

17. Finney, Charles G., *LECTURES TO PROFESSING CHRISTIANS* (New York, 1837)

18. Fleisch, Paul, *DIE MODERNE GEMEINSCHAFTSBEWEGUNG IN DEUTSCHLAND* (Leipzig, 1912)

19. SIX TRACTS BY W. B. GODBEY. *SPIRITUAL GIFTS AND GRACES* (Cincinnati, [1895]) *THE RETURN OF JESUS* (Cincinnati, [1899?]) *WORK OF THE HOLY SPIRIT* (Louisville, [1902]) *CHURCH—BRIDE—KINGDOM* (Cincinnati, [1905]) *DIVINE HEALING* (Greensboro, [1909]) *TONGUE MOVEMENT, SATANIC* (Zarephath, N. J., 1918)

20. Gordon, Earnest B., *ADONIRAM JUDSON GORDON* (New York, [1896])

21. Hills, A. M., *HOLINESS AND POWER FOR THE CHURCH AND THE MINISTRY* (Cincinnati, [1897])

22. Horner, Ralph C., *FROM THE ALTAR TO THE UPPER ROOM* (Toronto, [1891])

23. McDonald, William and John E. Searles, *THE LIFE OF REV. JOHN S. INSKIP* (Boston, [1885])

24. LaBerge, Agnes N. O., *WHAT GOD HATH WROUGHT* (Chicago, n. d.)

25. Lee, Luther, *AUTOBIOGRAPHY OF THE REV. LUTHER LEE* (New York, 1882)

26. McLean, A. and J. W. Easton, *PENUEL; OR, FACE TO FACE WITH GOD* (New York, 1869)

27. McPherson, Aimee Semple, *THIS IS THAT: PERSONAL EXPERIENCES SERMONS AND WRITINGS* (Los Angeles, [1919])

28. Mahan, Asa, *OUT OF DARKNESS INTO LIGHT* (London, 1877)

29. THE LIFE AND TEACHING OF CARRIE JUDD MONTGOMERY Carrie Judd Montgomery, *"UNDER HIS WINGS": THE STORY OF MY LIFE* (Oakland, [1936]) Carrie F. Judd, *THE PRAYER OF FAITH* (New York, 1880)

30. THE DEVOTIONAL WRITINGS OF PHOEBE PALMER Phoebe Palmer, *THE WAY OF HOLINESS* (52nd ed., New York, 1867) *FAITH AND ITS EFFECTS* (27th ed., New York, n. d., orig. pub. 1854)

31. Wheatley, Richard, *The Life and Letters of Mrs. Phoebe Palmer* (New York, 1881)

32. Palmer, Phoebe, ed., *Pioneer Experiences* (New York, 1868)

33. Palmer, Phoebe, *The Promise of the Father* (Boston, 1859)

34. Pardington, G. P., *Twenty-five Wonderful Years, 1889-1914: A Popular Sketch of the Christian and Missionary Alliance* (New York, [1914])

35. Parham, Sarah E., *The Life of Charles F. Parham, Founder of the Apostolic Faith Movement* (Joplin, [1930])

36. The Sermons of Charles F. Parham. Charles F. Parham, *A Voice Crying in the Wilderness* (4th ed., Baxter Springs, Kan., 1944, orig. pub. 1902) *The Everlasting Gospel* (n.p., n.d., orig. pub. 1911)

37. Pierson, Arthur Tappan, *Forward Movements of the Last Half Century* (New York, 1905)

38. *Proceedings of Holiness Conferences, Held at Cincinnati, November 26th, 1877, and at New York, December 17th, 1877* (Philadelphia, 1878)

39. *Record of the Convention for the Promotion of Scriptural Holiness Held at Brighton, May 29th, to June 7th, 1875* (Brighton, [1896?])

40. Rees, Seth Cook, *Miracles in the Slums* (Chicago, [1905?])

41. Roberts, B. T., *Why Another Sect* (Rochester, 1879)

42. Shaw, S. B., ed., *Echoes of the General Holiness Assembly* (Chicago, [1901])

43. The Devotional Writings of Robert Pearsall Smith and Hannah Whitall Smith. [R]obert [P]earsall [S]mith, *Holiness Through Faith: Light on the Way of Holiness* (New York, [1870]) [H]annah [W]hitall [S]mith, *The Christian's Secret of a Happy Life*, (Boston and Chicago, [1885])

44. [S]mith, [H]annah [W]hitall, *THE UNSELFISHNESS OF GOD AND HOW I DISCOVERED IT* (New York, [1903])

45. Steele, Daniel, *A SUBSTITUTE FOR HOLINESS; OR, ANTINOMIANISM REVIVED* (Chicago and Boston, [1899])

46. Tomlinson, A. J., *THE LAST GREAT CONFLICT* (Cleveland, 1913)

47. Upham, Thomas C., *THE LIFE OF FAITH* (Boston, 1845)

48. Washburn, Josephine M., *HISTORY AND REMINISCENCES OF THE HOLINESS CHURCH WORK IN SOUTHERN CALIFORNIA AND ARIZONA* (South Pasadena, [1912?])